S0-CYG-193

James
Stewart

James Stewart, as Mr Smith, arrives at his Washington office.

James Stewart

ALLAN HUNTER

 SPELLMOUNT LTD
Tunbridge Wells, Kent

 Hippocrene Books Inc
New York

First published in the UK in 1985 by
SPELLMOUNT LTD
12 Dene Way, Speldhurst
Tunbridge Wells, Kent TN3 ONX

ISBN 0-946771-81-2 (UK)

British Library Cataloguing in Publication Date
Hunter, Allan
James Stewart. – (Film and Theatre Stars)
1. Stewart, James 2. Actors –
United States – Biography
1. Title 2. Series

Published in the USA in 1985 by
Hippocrene Books Inc
171 Madison Avenue
New York, NY 10016

ISBN 0-87052-119-5 (USA)

Commissioning Editor: Sue Rolfe
Design: Sue Ryall

Printed & bound in Great Britain by
Biddles Ltd, Guildford, Surrey.

Contents

Acknowledgements are due to the following for the pictures that appear on the pages indicated:

MGM: 2, 12, 24a; Universal City Studios: 3, 48-9 (*RW* and *Vertigo*), 61; Cathay Center Distibutors: 4, 66; Columbia Pictures: frontispiece, 24b; The Kobal Collection: 24a (MGM), 26 (Paramount), 33 (RKO), cover; National Film Archive: frontispiece, 29, 41, 45-6; World Wide: 38; Grand Nation Pictures: 40; Paramount: 26, 44, 48 (TMWKTM), 59; Universal Pictures: 64-5, 68; Warner Bros.: 60 CBS: 67 CIC: 68.

List of Illustrations

7

Introduction

'I am James Stewart, playing James Stewart. I couldn't mess around doing great characterisations. I play variations of myself. Audiences have come to expect certain things from me and are disappointed if they don't get them.' That typically modest statement from one of the 'living legends' of Hollywood masks a considerable talent and a popularity that have sustained James Stewart through half a century of film stardom.

For Stewart it really has been a wonderful life. A Princeton graduate in architecture, his early attachment to the acting profession amounted to little more than the casual interest of a passing fancy. Now, his standing as one of the best actors to emerge from the golden years of Hollywood is unassailable. He has given moviegoers a score of indelible impressions that readily come to mind and a thousand images that provide a shorthand summation of a career: an idealistic young senator striving to uphold the values in which he believes; a popular musician looking for his individual sound; a genial dipsomaniac with an oversize rabbit for a best friend; a sad circus clown with a secret; a cagey, small-town lawyer; and, perhaps paramount, images of a man of the West, slow to anger but lethal when roused.

The name James Stewart above a film's title has always signalled certain qualities of integrity, decency, humanity and sincerity. Audiences find it natural to identify with his stumbling, slow-talking heroics, comfortable in the knowledge that his dogged efforts and fallibility will eventually win through. The director Frank Capra has said: 'He had some of the qualities that Gary Cooper had. That

9

James Stewart – MGM portrait from the 1930s.

With Alfred Hitchcock on the set of Rear Window *(1954).*

The Cheyenne Social Club *(1970) with old friend and co-star Henry Fonda, and director Gene Kelly.*

indefinable personal integrity—awfully hard to make Jimmy look bad.' A fellow veteran, Henry Hathaway, has observed: 'There's two kinds of actors. There's the kind that are natural-born-for-what-they-are-actors. John Wayne is a natural-born strong man, he just looks, he's strong. Cooper was a gentle man but strong. They're born with these kind of things—Henry Fonda and Jimmy Stewart are born with it, it's nothing they learned in school or from the stage or experience, except that they learned to have confidence. Now there's other actors that learn techniques. They're the worst ones. As soon as they've learned techniques on how to do certain things, then it's not them.'

When Stewart arrived on the Hollywood scene his lanky, unsophisticated figure possessed few of the conventional attributes required for screen stardom. His looks hardly classified him as the matinee idol type represented by Robert Taylor or Tyrone Power, neither did he have the rugged brawn of a Gable and, whilst boyish, he was a little too mature to satisfy the American public's appetite for juveniles as evidenced in the popularity of Mickey Rooney. Stewart did not fit any of the prevailing pigeon-holes, and thus he created a niche of his own—the boy next door. It was an image which, through time and maturity, would develop into that of everyone's favourite uncle or the father they wished had been their own. Louella Parsons believed him to be 'the most nearly normal of all Hollywood stars'. Audiences found the deceptive simplicity of his naturalism so arresting that they took some convincing that what Stewart did could be termed acting. Cary Grant, Stewart's co-star in *The Philadelphia Story* and a close friend, is convinced that Stewart provided a prototype in screen acting that influenced succeeding generations.

Grant once said: 'Cyclically speaking Jimmy Stewart had the same effect on pictures that Marlon Brando had some years later. Jimmy had the ability to talk naturally. He knew that in conversation people *do* often interrupt one another and that it's not always so easy to get a thought out. It took a little while for the soundmen to get used to him, but he had an enormous impact. And then, some years later, Marlon came out and did the same thing all over again—but what people forget is that Jimmy did it first. And he affected all of us really.'

Stewart has carefully engineered both his screen image and his career, 'I have my own rules and adhere to them', he claims. 'The rule is simple but inflexible—a Jimmy Stewart picture must have two

11

vital ingredients: it will be clean and it will involve the triumph of the underdog over the bully. I like the character of the vulnerable man. The man who plods around and things aren't easy for him, he's indecisive and troubled. But he has faith, determination and courage. I think human frailty is a very nice thing to portray.' Stewart also has a philosophy of acting: 'The most important thing in motion picture acting is that you try to develop a character and do it so the acting doesn't show and if you're successful in doing this, then believability starts sneaking in, and if you start to get people believing in what you're doing up there on the screen then you're in pretty good shape.' His life-long friend Henry Fonda offered a simple but succinct appreciation of Stewart: 'He's an instinctual actor who started out being good, learned his craft and became great'.

Stewart himself summed up his thoughts on movies in a 1966 interview with Peter Bogdanovich. *'This is the great thing that the movies have,' he said, 'the potential to really press things home *visually*—they come closer than anything else, the people can see your *eyes*. . . they can – I remember we were up in Canada in 1954 in the mountains shooting a picture called *The Far Country*. We were havin' a bawx lunch—the usual terrible bawx lunch—and this old guy came into the camp. . . and looked around. . . he looked. . . and he came over t'me. . . nawdded at me. 'You Stewart?' 'Yeah' 'You did a thing in a picture once', he said. 'Can't remember the name of it – but you were in a room – and you said a poem or something 'bout fireflies. . . That was good.' 'I knew right away what he meant – that's all he said—he was talking about a scene in a picture called *Come Live With Me* that came out in 1941—and he couldn't remember the title, but that little. . . tiny thing – didn't last even a minute—he'd remembered all those years. . . An' *that's* the thing – that's the great thing about movies. . . After you *learn*—and if you're good and Gawd helps ya and you're lucky enough to have a personality that comes across—then what you're doing is. . . you're giving people little. . . little, tiny pieces of *time*. . . that they never forget.'

This book is both an examination and celebration of the countless, unforgettable 'little, tiny pieces of time' that make up the career of James Stewart.

---

*The author and interviewer here attempts to capture James Stewart's speech pattern on paper. See Select bibliography.

Chapter 1

James Maitland Stewart was born on Wednesday 20 May, 1908 in the town of Indiana, a small community in Pennsylvania with a population of under eight thousand people. Stewart's mother Elizabeth Ruth Jackson, liked to call her first-born Jimsy. His father, Alexander Stewart, described by James himself as a 'big, brusque sort of Irish man', preferred 'Jimbo'.

The Stewarts were solid, respectable members of the Indiana community. His father ran the local hardware store which had been founded in 1853 by his paternal grandfather. The family were regular churchgoers, Elizabeth was involved in the Ladies' Aid and Alexander was a member of the Volunteer Fire Department. In later years Stewart commented: 'This is where I sort of made up my mind about certain things; about hard work being worth it, about community spirit, about the importance of family, about the importance of God and the church'. The values instilled into Stewart as a child were to become paramount in the shaping of his screen image.

Stewart was a child with an inquisitive mind, eager to find out what made things tick. He dabbled in chemistry, he built crystal radio sets with a little help from his father, he constructed model aeroplanes and thus began a life-long fascination with aviation. He was also a dab hand at parlour tricks and sleight of hand which fostered an ambition to be a magician. He was a member of the local Boy Scout troop and during the First World War, with his father in the army, he devised a number of plays which displayed his patriotic fervour. As writer and performer his shows included 'To Hell with the Kaiser' and 'The

Slacker'. Often he would be helped and hindered in his fledgling acting efforts by his baby sisters Mary, born in 1912, and Virginia, born in 1914.

Stewart's father ran a hardware store where, if a customer could not afford to pay cash, suitable alternative arrangements could be made. A system of barter developed, and once an impoverished group of circus performers paid in kind by leaving a pet python to cover their purchases. Another item received into the Stewart household in this way was an accordion. Young James soon gained a proficiency with the instrument and played in the Scout band.

Stewart's education began at the Model School and continued at Mercersburg Academy where he excelled at athletics. He became fully engaged by non-academic pursuits: singing in the choir, acting in the senior play and playing his accordion in the school orchestra. Stewart's father had attended Princeton University and James was expected to follow him, then come into the hardware store. He graduated from Mercersburg in 1928 and duly headed for Princeton, although initially somewhat confused as to where his true academic interests lay. He began with a major in civil engineering, and later changed to steam engineering, but a poor grasp of mathematics held him back. He tried political studies but eventually settled in as an architectural student, emerging four years later as a Bachelor of Science.

It was while he was at Princeton that Stewart became side-tracked into acting. He had no desperate yearning to enter the theatre and would certainly not have viewed the prospect as providing a stable future for a smalltown boy. At Princeton he became involved in the Triangle Club and in 1928 he appeared in one of their shows entitled *The Golden Dog*, written by Al Wade and Joshua Logan. Logan would go on to find fame as the director of hit shows and films like *Mister Roberts* and *South Pacific*. Writing in his autobiography he recalled the 'lanky, drawling sophomore' and stated, 'one of the young accordion players who was in a number called "Blue Hell" had an attractive personality and I asked him if he ever thought of becoming an actor. "Good God, no. I'm going to be an architect." He walked away as if I had slandered him. His name was James Stewart.'

Stewart continued to be convinced that his calling was architecture, but gradually the enjoyment of performing in plays and entertaining on the accordion exerted a stronger hold. He appeared in the

14

Triangle Club Christmas show performing an accordion solo and, in 1930, played in *The Tiger Smiles Again* with Joshua Logan. Also, during the vacations he had worked out an act with a friend, Bill Neff, and was able to tour his home territory entertaining the folks with a mixture of music and magic. During Stewart's final year he acted as stage manager for a production of *The Artist and the Lady* which proved important in gaining him an introduction to the leading lady-guest artiste, Margaret Sullavan. She had been in the University Players, a summer stock group, with Logan and struck up a strong and lasting friendship with Stewart.

Stewart graduated in 1932, intending to continue his studies and gain his Master's degree. Logan intervened and offered him a job. Logan's University Players company had settled for another summer at West Falmouth on Cape Cod. Logan offered Stewart the chance to join the periphery of the company, taking an occasional role in their productions and playing the accordion at the adjoining Old Silver Black Tea Room. Stewart's first roles with the company came in a revival of Booth Tarkington's comedy *Magnolia* and in Laurence E.Johnston's *It's A Wise Child*.

Joshua Logan knew that Stewart had the ability and personality to try for a career in the theatre, and he believes that Stewart felt the same way but 'was too embarrassed to admit it'. After graduating, however, Stewart had to make a firm choice between the stage or continuing his studies. Princeton offered him a scholarship which would have enabled him to commence a post-graduate course, but after much deliberation he declined their offer, feeling that a further period at university would place an unnecessary burden on the family finances especially as both his sisters by now were also students. Mary had chosen an art course at Carnegie Tech and Virginia was headed for Vassar. Stewart wrote to his parents to explain the path he had chosen.

Later Stewart would say; 'I was interested in architecture. But I guess I wasn't interested enough. I really did want to become an architect, but nobody was putting up any buildings at the time. Yet the theatre was exploding: there was a tremendous activity, a kind of reaction against the Depression. So many fine comedians were to develop in those years—Bob Hope, W.C.Fields, Bill Robinson. I think all my contemporaries would agree that we were particularly fortunate to have cut our teeth in the theatre at that time.' In 1932 however Stewart was still not convinced that he had made the right decision and would say; 'Acting is no job for a man. You work two hours a night, *when you work*; and you sleep all morning and maybe all day because you have nothing else to do.' He need not have worried; the acting profession may have conjured up an image of insecurity and high unemployment, but the young James Stewart proved a glorious exception to the generalisations, and in the event scarcely suffered a day of enforced unemployment in over half a century.

Joshua Logan involved the University Players in a business arrangement with the Broadway producer Arthur J.Beckhard. The first fruit of their collaboration saw the participation of Logan's group in the play *Carrie Nation* which starred Beckhard's wife Esther Dale in the title role as the famed temperance campaigner. The play was tried out in West Falmouth and Baltimore before heading for Broadway where it opened at the Biltmore Theatre on 29 October 1932. Logan described the reviews as 'deservedly lugubrious' and the show ran for a mere thirty-one performances. However, it did provide the Broadway debut of Stewart in the role of Constable Gano.

Beckhard's second assault on Broadway, the comedy *Goodbye Again*, was much more successful, opening in December 1932 and running for over two hundred performances. Stewart played the chauffeur in Act One, a small role of short duration but the audiences responded appreciatively. One reviewer in the New York *Sun* noted, 'It seems apropos to say a few words about James Stewart, a player in this mad piece, who is on the stage for exactly three minutes and speaks no more than eight lines. Yet before this gentleman exits he makes a definite impression on audiences because he makes them laugh so hard'.

Stewart earned a handsome thirty-five dollars a week for his part in *Goodbye Again* and decided to join with Logan and another friend, pool their resources and set up a bachelor apartment in West Sixty-Third Street off Central Park. Later they were joined by a young, out-of-work actor named Henry Fonda. Their neighbourhood was hardly the most salubrious, and Fonda declared it 'full of gangsters, whores and pimps', while the famed racketeer Legs Diamond based himself nearby. Once a week the four friends hosted a 'Beer Club' and invited over neighbours like Burgess Meredith and colleagues and friends like Margaret Sullavan, Benny Goodman and Mildred Natwick.

When *Goodbye Again* closed Stewart did not lack offers. He was engaged as the stage manager for the Boston run of *Camille*, starring Jane Cowl, and returned to New York to carry out the same task for *Spring in Autumn*, starring Blanche Yurka. In the latter he also essayed a small role as Jack Breenan. When Logan went on a trip to Russia and the 'Beer Club' quartet went their separate ways Stewart and Fonda moved into the Madison Square Hotel and were both engaged for the comedy *All Good Americans*, earning fifty dollars a week each.

In 1934 Stewart's ever inquisitive mind led him to investigate the world of the cinema. It was not the technical side of film-making that engaged his mind so much as the rumoured salary of fifty dollars a day. Thus he appeared in *Art Trouble*, a two-reel Warner Brothers comedy shot in a Long Island studio, which more than satisfied his curiosity.

Having been active in the theatre world of Broadway for two years now, Stewart was much less convincing when trying to shrug acting off as an enjoyable diversion. In 1934 he was cast as the idealistic, self-sacrificing Sergeant O'Hara in Sidney Kingsley's *Yellow Jack* which, he believes, was 'the turning point of my work on stage'. Stewart, working with a skilled director, Guthrie McClintic, was beginning to feel the rapport between performer and audience and experience the many satisfactions of his chosen art. His name appeared in lights for the first time, his work was well received by critics, and the show ran a modest seventy-nine performances. It also brought him to the attention of Billy Grady, a talent scout for the film studio Metro-Goldwyn-Mayer.

Stewart spent the summer of 1934 working with the Locust Valley Company at the Red Barn Theatre on the north shore of Long Island. He returned to New York, working again with Guthrie McClintic, to play Teddy Parish in *Divided By Three* which starred Judith Anderson. The play was short-lived but Stewart's notices were good. His friend Henry Fonda noted with some awe how accomplished Stewart had become: 'I went to the opening night and afterwards in his dressing room I remember just sitting, looking at him and studying him and wondering how the hell he got to be so good! You see, I'd been at it for eight or nine years, already playing literally hundreds of parts of all kinds and really working at being an actor, and here was this skinny son-of-a-bitch who hadn't really tried very hard for maybe a year or so and I'd just seen him do about the most moving job I've ever seen in the theatre.' The company of *Divided By Three* also included Hedda Hopper who is reputed to have advised MGM to consider putting Stewart under contract.

Stewart had been screen-tested by Twentieth-Century Fox, an experience he recalls as 'one of those watch-the-horses-run affairs — you gravely turn your head from one side to the other, and assume that you're observing something intently'. MGM's Billy Grady arranged a screen-test in New York with Stewart performing a scene from *Divided By Three*, but the studio bosses back in Culver City hesitated over whether to sign this lanky newcomer.

Stewart next appeared in the farce *Page Miss Glory*, directed by George Abbott, which opened in November 1934; and, his last stage stage work for some years, *Journey By Night*, appeared briefly in April 1935 at the Schubert Theatre. The show managed seven performances. Stewart was cast, or rather miscast, as a Viennese bank clerk who turns to crime. His work was savaged by the critics but he claimed that he had badly needed the money. However, with the strong support of Billy Grady, MGM at last came through with the offer of a contract for three months, with renewal options.

James Stewart arrived in Hollywood in 1935 and joined Henry Fonda who had already gone west to film his Broadway success *The Farmer Takes A Wife*. The two young hopefuls rented a Mexican-style farmhouse in Brentwood, where Greta Garbo happened to be their next-door neighbour, and Stewart reported for work at Culver City.

Chapter 2

In 1935 Americans were going to the movies at the rate of eighty million admissions per week and Metro-Goldwyn-Mayer had recorded net profits in excess of $7 million for the past two years. MGM was the studio that boasted a roster of 'more stars than there are in the heavens' and in 1935 their biggest box-office names were Joan Crawford and Clark Gable, the latter having just been awarded an Oscar for Columbia's *It Happened One Night*.

Stewart's first assignment at Metro incongruously cast the six-foot-three-and-a-half-inch actor as 'Shorty', a fledgling newspaper reporter colleague of the star, Spencer Tracy, in *The Murder Man*. The film was of little significance although it did mark Tracy's first film under his new contract with MGM, a studio which would be his working home for the next twenty years. Tracy plays a newspaperman, Steve Grey, who kills one of two men responsible for his wife's suicide and fakes the evidence to implicate the other. Eventually his basic decency causes him to confess his 'perfect crime'. Stewart, listed ninth in the cast, went largely unheralded but his own assessment of his performance was, 'I was awful. I was all arms and legs'.

Stewart's contract with MGM was renewed nonetheless, and he was kept busy working out in the gym and also, in his spare time, gaining his pilot's licence. In 1936 his talents were exercised and stretched, with his work on view in eight feature films. *Rose Marie* was released in January, an unplanned reunion for Nelson Eddy and Jeanette MacDonald who had first appeared together in *Naughty Marietta* the previous year. The Metropolitan opera star Grace Moore

19

'Hardly the matinee idol type.'

was originally scheduled to appear opposite Nelson Eddy but concert commitments forced her withdrawal and the replacement casting of Jeanette MacDonald. She plays Marie Flower, a haughty Canadian opera singer who only shows affection to her wastrel brother John (Stewart), a prisoner. Her affections are sorely tried when John escapes from jail, killing a mountie in the process. The injured John hides out in the lake country and Marie hurries to comfort him. En route she meets and falls in love with the mountie Sergeant Bruce (Eddy) who is in pursuit of her brother. Bruce does his duty and John is subsequently executed, but the love between the mountie and the singer flourishes.

Rose Marie was a popular hit which presented Stewart to a wide public in a role of some substance and, this time, his presence was favourably noted by critics. The shy twenty-seven year-old remained level-headed about the attention, however, commenting, 'Hollywood dishes out too much praise for small things like my role in *Rose Marie*. I won't let it get to me, but too much praise can turn a fellow's head if he doesn't watch his step'.

Margaret Sullavan, Stewart's friend from the University Players and Fonda's ex-wife, had also made her way to Hollywood and signed an advantageous contract with Universal which incorporated a starting salary of $1200 a week. When the studio was searching for a suitable co-star for a film of Ursula Pratt's novel *Next Time We Live* she specifically requested Stewart and he was duly borrowed from Metro. The resulting film, entitled *Next Time We Love*, proved a three-handkerchief soap-opera on the theme of marriage versus career. Sullavan plays an actress, Cicely Tyler, married to Stewart's journalist Chris, and the film charts their sacrifices as both pursue their individual careers to the detriment of their once blissful union. Happiness is once more restored as Sullavan rushes to Europe to help Stewart recover from a serious illness contracted in China and vows 'next time we live, we'll have time for each other'.

A somewhat clichéd film *Next Time We Love* nevertheless benefits from the fresh, appealing understatement of the lead performancees and the obvious warmth and tenderness in the rapport between Stewart and Sullavan. Stewart received favourable reviews for this, his first substantial screen role, and *Time* magazine prophetically noted: 'The chief significance of *Next Time We Love* in the progress of the cinema industry is likely to reside in the presence in its cast of

21

James Stewart . . . He disregards a long established cinema convention for such roles, and ably introduces to Hollywood the character of a newspaper man who is neither drunkard, lecher nor buffoon'.

Stewart returned to Metro and a couple of assignments in support of the studio's more established names. In *Small Town Girl* he plays Elmer, the 'other' man and small-town boyfriend of Janet Gaynor, who loses his girl not once but twice to doctor Robert Taylor. More satisfying for Stewart was *Wife Versus Secretary*, which wound up as one of the year's most popular films, thanks to the potent chemistry of Clark Gable, Myrna Loy and Jean Harlow. Gable is a magazine publisher, Van Sanford, who loves his wife Linda (Loy); however the demands of his job find him innocently spending more time with his pretty secretary, Whitney (Harlow). A jealous wife suspects they are having an affair but is persuaded otherwise and Whitney is content with her long-suffering boyfriend Dave (Stewart). Stewart had cause to recall the film because, as he described his memorable encounter with Harlow: 'When Harlow kissed you, she *kissed* you'. The film's director, Clarence Brown, later said, 'I guess in my day the thinking was that to make a picture all you needed was to take a little shop girl and wind up with her married to the governor of the state. The true-to-life shop girl goes to see the picture and thinks, "Maybe I can do that too". But I guess the real key to my success was love stories. You can't miss with a triangle love story. When you put on a billboard, *Wife Versus Secretary* with Harlow the harlot, Loy the wife and Gable the man, you don't need a story. You've got all you need right there.'

Metro next entrusted Stewart with his first starring vehicle, a B-feature entitled *Speed* in which he portrays a test driver, Terry Martin, who is developing a new high-speed carburetor. It is a simple tale of man and machine, and man and boss's daughter, with the man winding up with both by the film's conclusion. *Speed* was simple studio fodder designed to keep the factory line ticking over, and after that for Stewart it was back to supporting roles: as one of Joan Crawford's many male admirers in the stilted historical drama *The Gorgeous Hussy* (a role once intended for Jean Harlow); and as the unexpected villain in the sparkling murder mystery *After the Thin Man*, a worthy successor to the studio's 1934 hit and reuniting William Powell, Myrna Loy and Asta the terrier. Stewart correctly assessed why he had been cast in the latter film. 'You know what happens in that kind of whodunnit thing. They made me the heavy because I was the one the audience was supposed to suspect the least.' Nevertheless the unveiling of the shy, callow Stewart as the murderer of his former lover's husband provided an effective twist ending.

Stewart's fortunate casting in the musical *Born to Dance* came late in the development of a project that was intended to display the terpsichorean talents of Eleanor Powell. The plot was within the well-tried formula of sailors on shore leave and their amorous encounters. Stewart was seen as a gauche officer, Ted Barker, who meets an aspiring dancer, Nora Paige (Powell). The path of their love runs across some unwelcome bumps before Nora achieves Broadway success and Ted wins her heart. Stewart won the role at the suggestion of the composer, Cole Porter, here writing his first score for MGM. The studio acceded to his suggestion and Stewart went to audition for Porter who wrote, 'He sings far from well, although he has nice notes in his voice, but he could play the part perfectly'. Stewart stepped forward both to dance and sing in the film and, whilst Fred Astaire could rest easy over the competition, he brings a husky sincerity to his one big number 'Easy to Love', a romantic highlight sung to Eleanor Powell on a park bench. Years later Stewart recalled: 'You almost didn't hear me sing that song. I had no pretensions as a singer, but I thought I got through it rather well. And then, when the film was finished, we all went off to Long Beach for a sneak preview, and I discovered that my song was sung by someone else: they had dubbed in a 'real' singer. I was disappointed but no more . . I had no ambitions as a singer, so I thought — who cares?

'Then, coming back from the hugely successful preview, the moguls decided that the scene was so good, and the song such a success, that even I couldn't kill it, so my voice was dubbed back into the scene.'

Born to Dance was one of the studio's most popular releases of the year and proved a useful step up the ladder for Stewart, although there were some critics who demurred, notably Alistair Cooke: 'There is James Stewart trying to be ingenuous and charming like Gary Cooper but many tricks and years behind!'

In 1936 Stewart also appeared in a ten-minute MGM short *Important News* opposite Chic Sale. It had been a year of intense activity for him, of gaining experience and immersing himself in acquiring the

23

skills of acting for the camera. Despite his obvious successes and the projection of a personality with which audiences could identify, the MGM top brass remained oblivious to his potential. No-one at the studio was able to see the star material before their eyes and seemed content merely to extract full employment value from their Broadway import. Perhaps the policy of 'more stars than the heavens' stifled their urge to promote new ones. Be that as it may, Metro appeared satisfied with Stewart as a supporting actor, useful for country bumpkin characterisations. Some of the talents on the MGM lot displayed more discretion, however; for example, director Robert Z. Leonard was filming *The Great Ziegfeld* and received an offer of Stewart's services for a very minor role. He refused, saying he 'wouldn't want to spoil his future by putting him in a bit role'. But Metro continued to entertain bizarre notions of the kind of roles for which Stewart might be suitable; at one stage he was sent for a test with Paul Muni for the part of Ching in the film of Pearl Buck's *The Good Earth*. Stewart later told Peter Bogdanovich: 'They gawt me all made up — took all morning — an' gawt me together with Paul Muni and . . there was just . . just one thing . . wrong . . I was too *tall!* *So they dug a trench* and I walked in it and Muni walked alongside . . . an' I . . . I didn't get the part. I didn't . . . They gave the part to a Chinaman!'

Metro's uncertainty in handling the actor's career, however, seemed not to faze him at all. In many ways he was having the time of his life, as he said almost half a century later: 'Life in 1936 was wonderful. You were working everyday including Saturdays. Sometimes I was working on three films at a time. You learned the craft of acting by *acting*, by working on films.' His bachelor life with Henry Fonda was fine too as the duo double-dated with the likes of Lucille Ball and Ginger Rogers whilst Stewart tried to distance himself from the lavish attentions of Norma Shearer. The small-town boy was even finding his own sense of community in the reputedly impersonal world of Hollywood, developing friendships with Humphrey Bogart and his screen co-stars. 'The whole set-up in Hollywood was such that you'd get about half stuck on your leading lady or some gal in the picture, and they'd generally turn out to be your dates. Every Saturday night we'd go over to the Trocadero or the Coconut Grove. They were wonderful sorts of nightclubs. We didn't get very good tables because the maitre d's didn't know who we were.

'They stayed open all night and the most famous people just got up and performed — Mary and Jack Benny, George Burns and Gracie Allen, Red Skelton, and I remember one night Judy Garland's mother brought her. Judy wore pigtails and bobby sox and she sang for an hour. Absolutely terrific! I don't know why people have the impression that California is a cold, unfriendly place. There was a real sort of camaraderie, and Hank and I had great times.'

After the hectic pace of filming in 1936 Stewart was seen in, by comparison, a modest three productions in 1937. The first to be released was *Seventh Heaven*, a remake of the silent success which had starred Janet Gaynor and Charles Farrell. MGM had loaned Stewart to Twentieth-Century Fox for the film when that studio hurriedly sought a replacement for Tyrone Power. Perhaps the most charitable comment to be made on *Seventh Heaven* is that Stewart was miscast. The part of Chico, a Parisian sewer worker brimming with confidence in his own worth and perennially striking a poetic note, hardly seems the best showcase for Stewart's special abilities. Simone Simon stars as Diane, the street waif in whose arms he finds love until war separates them. Her belief in his safe return sustains her through four years until he does return having lost his sight. Stewart did not attempt a French accent and the film was a flop. After that, and back at Metro, he was in *The Last Gangster* in which Edward G.Robinson is conventionally cast as a jailed gangster whose wife divorces him and marries journalist Stewart, the latter adopting the gangster's son. Ten years later Robinson is back on the streets seeking vengeance but is impressed enough by the Stewart household to leave well alone. Later he is slain by another mobster. *The Last Gangster* was an unusual film to emerge from MGM as most of the major works in the ganster genre had originated from Warner Brothers; *The Last Gangster* did nothing to reverse that trend. A moustachioed Stewart is effectively used to signify decent respectability and the New York *Herald Tribune* found him, 'casually right as the nice fellow'.

Navy, Blue and Gold was much more successful. It concentrated on the adventures of a trio of roommates at Annapolis and their quest to excel at football. The trio are Robert Young, Stewart and Tom Brown in a tale of honour and camaraderie ending in an important football game that is won by the co-ordinated efforts of Young and Stewart. The New York *Herald Tribune* again championed Stewart's work: 'It is due to his expert rendition of a rather preposterous part that a rather preposterous show becomes generally exciting'.

Stewart also found himself employed on radio in 1937. MGM and Maxwell House coffee combined to produce an hour-long show, *Good News*, to promote their products. The regular host was Robert Young, but during his absence Stewart substituted as the presenter. Stewart also made appearances on a Sunday afternoon series called *The Silver Theatre* and was heard opposite Ann Harding in a Lux Radio Theatre production of *Madame X*. MGM may not have been sure how to show Stewart to his best advantage but they were certainly not keeping him idle. This experience of all sorts of different work was crucial to him and exciting opportunities for advancement were just around the corner.

Chapter 3

Of Human Hearts, directed by Clarence Brown, was the first of four films featuring Stewart that appeared in 1938. An impressive piece of Americana, it provided an authentic and winning picture of a backwoods family in nineteenth-century Ohio which neither caricatured nor satirised the people depicted. Walter Huston stars as Ethan Wilkins, a stern, God-fearing minister who is perplexed by the actions of his son Jason (Stewart). Jason rebels against his father's principles and runs away from home to study medicine. Following his father's death Jason's mother Mary (Beulah Bondi) makes endless sacrifices to support him through his studies. During the Civil War Jason is a highly valued surgeon but neglects his mother who assumes that he has been killed. Mary writes to President Lincoln (John Carradine) asking the location of her son's grave and the President summons the gifted young surgeon, lectures him on his unthinking ingratitude and sends him on leave to visit his mother.

Of Human Hearts is not bereft of sentimentality but it gains strength from the simple human dignity which is invested in the characters by Stewart, Huston and Bondi. Stewart faced a challenging task in illuminating the stubbornness of a boy who rejects the values of his father and ultimately ignores the love of his mother. He convincingly captured those moods in a characterisation of some sensitivity.

At RKO, in *Vivacious Lady*, Stewart was able to reveal a hitherto untapped penchant for comedy and display his versatility. Here Stewart plays Peter Morgan, a botany professor who visits New York and falls head over heels in love with a nightclub entertainer, Francey (Ginger Rogers). Acting on impulse the couple marry and face endless complications as the professor and wife return to face the stuffy world of academe and Morgan's own inability to break the news to his father, a stickler for respectability. Eventually, of course, the new Mrs Morgan gains acceptance on campus, for *Vivacious Lady* is a light, frothy situation-comedy using the classic formula of the ill-matched odd couple and outraged conventions. The director, George Stevens, later summed up Stewart's qualities which had led him to borrow the actor from MGM: 'The boy and the girl had no business getting together — so the movie was really about the pleasant frustration of non-communication. This was very close to Jimmy Stewart's vein of expression — this struggle to get anything said. Now, to overcome disbelief is the most difficult thing to do in films. And Jimmy, with this extraordinary earnestness he had, just walked in and extinguished disbelief'.

Stewart returned to Metro for a rather flat remake of *The Shopworn Angel*, previously filmed in 1929 with Gary Cooper and Nancy Carroll in the roles now played by Stewart and Margaret Sullavan. Stewart is Private Bill Pettigrew, a simple fellow from Texas en route to the trenches of France in World War 1, who encounters a stage star, Daisy Heath (Sullavan). He is deeply enamoured of her glamour and sophistication while she responds to his naivety and obvious sincerity. She returns his affection despite her involvement with her manager Sam Bailey (Walter Pidgeon). To avoid hurting his feelings Daisy agrees to marry Bill and their union takes place on the eve of his departure. He is killed in action, allowing Daisy and Sam to be reunited.

The mawkishness inherent in *The Shopworn Angel* is largely avoided by the depth of conviction brought to their roles by Sullavan and Stewart, the latter being particularly effective as the bashful soldier. The film received fine notices from contemporary reviewers and Stewart was often singled out for praise as in the New York *Herald Tribune* of 18 July 1938: 'James Stewart brings the Texan private to glowing life and keeps the characterisation solid and appealing even when the script gives him little aid. Unless I am mistaken, *The Shopworn Angel* boasts two of the finest actors appearing on the screen today'.

More satisfying for the long-term development of Stewart's career, however, was Columbia's *You Can't Take It With You*, his first film for director Frank Capra and another instance of the actor finding his best opportunities outside the confines of his home studio. Based on the Pulitzer prize-winning Broadway comedy by George S. Kaufman and Moss Hart, the play made ideal material for Capra who used it as a vehicle to celebrate the importance of individuality and the liberty of everyone to do their own thing. Capra's film is literally crammed with humanity bursting at the seams to express themselves. Lionel Barrymore plays Grandpa Vanderhof, a retired businessman and happy host to his family and many eccentric friends. Grandpa is being pressurised to sell his home to an acquisitive, stuffed-shirt businessman Mr Kirby (Edward Arnold). Whilst the older generation are at odds with each other the younger generation of Grandpa's granddaughter Alice (Jean Arthur) and Kirby's son Tony (Stewart) are falling in love. The resentment and discomfort of two opposing philosophies are reconciled in their love and Kirby Senior ultimately proves himself to be human after all.

You Can't Take It With You was one of the year's big comedy successes, winning two Oscars for Capra as the producer and the director of the 'Best Film Of 1938'. Stewart faced a fairly undemanding task as the juvenile lead who forms one part of the broad canvas of Capra's film, but it did his career no harm at all for him to be found in such a popular venture.

Stewart was now approaching the peak period in his pre-war film work. 1939, indeed represents something of an *annus mirabilis* in both his career and the output of the major Hollywood studios. Of Stewart's five releases in 1939 two were to become classics of Hollywood's Golden era, two are distinguished examples of their type, and one sank deservedly into oblivion.

Made for Each other appeared on American screens just before St Valentine's Day in 1939, appropriate timing as the subject-matter centred around the trials and tribulations in the true love of a couple of newlyweds. Stewart is a young attorney, Johnny Mason, whose impulsive marriage to Jane (Carole Lombard) takes some explaining to his mother and the girl he was expected to marry — his boss's daughter. Easy-going and rather weak-willed Johnny seems to lack the backbone to make a go of his marriage — he is unable to stand up to his bossy mother and, at work, accepts a pay cut and the loss of a promotion that is due to him. Johnny believes himself unworthy of his bride but the couple are reunited when their child is critically ill with pneumonia. A life-saving serum is flown through a blizzard from Salt Lake City to New York and the whole incident infuses Johnny with the resolve to confront his bosses, improve his lot and live happily ever after with Jane.

The melodramatic climax of *Made for Each Other* tends to undermine an otherwise convincingly handled soap-opera. Although Lombard is top-billed her unusually dramatic role is somewhat subservient to Stewart's unsympathetic underdog. At least the film has more to commend it than Stewart's next venture, *Ice Follies of 1939*.

Stewart was now acceptable leading man material around most of the major studios, and with co-stars like Ginger Rogers and Carole Lombard his own star was indeed in the ascendant. The latter fact must have seemed obvious to everyone expect MGM who again displayed little idea of how to utilise effectively a performer who, after all, was under contract to them. The studio had scheduled him to co-star with Robert Taylor in 'Hands Across the Border', a project which never advanced beyond a script. With *Ice Follies of 1939* the studio seemed intent on sabotaging the careers of the three leading protagonists — Stewart, Lew Ayres, and Joan Crawford whose box-office allure had temporarily waned. The plot, of career versus personal happiness, was only incidental to the ice-skating sequences and perhaps Metro hoped to acquire some of the audience who avidly awaited the acrobatics of Sonja Henie. Joan Crawford later admitted, 'Everyone went out of their creative minds when they made *Ice Follies*. Me, Jimmy Stewart and Lew Ayres as skaters . . . preposterous. A dancer I am, a skater I'm not . . . It was a catastrophe. The public thought so too.' Writing in her autobiography Crawford revealed, 'I adored working with Jimmy. He's such an endearing character, a perfectionist at his job, but with a droll sense of humour and a shy way of watching to see if you react to that humour'.

MGM finally unearthed for Stewart a comparatively worthy script *It's A Wonderful World*, a screwball comedy co-starring Claudette Colbert. A highly diverting piece of nonsense, the film allowed Stewart a free rein to explore the comic potential in his role. He plays Guy Johnson, a novice detective, who acts as a 'minder' to a millionaire playboy. When the latter is unjustly accused of murder Guy is named as an accessory. He escapes from custody, hoping to find the real killer. He steals a car and unwittingly kidnaps the

30

With Claudette Colbert in the zany comedy It's a Wonderful World.

With Jean Arthur in Frank Capra's Mr Smith goes to Washington.

vehicle's owner, poet Edwina Corday (Colbert). The two make an unlikely team but prove triumphant, unmasking the real villain and falling in love in the process. The film is unpretentious, wild and woolly fun with Stewart called upon to enact various disguises, among them that of a chauffeur, an actor and a Boy Scout leader. It was his next film, however, which brought him into full stardom.

For *Mr Smith Goes to Washington* Stewart went back to Columbia, and back to Frank Capra. Capra once claimed: 'I wanted to glorify the average man, not the guy at the top, not the politician, not the banker, just the ordinary guy whose strength I admire, whose survivability I admire'. Stewart's character of Jefferson Smith is an ordinary man whose ideals and whose survivability are tested to the limit.

Smith is a respected Montana citizen and head of the local Boy Rangers. To a corrupt party machine he is slow-witted and susceptible; the ideal voting fodder who won't make waves and can serve out the remaining term of office of a recently departed Senator. Smith is appointed to the Senate, carefully watched over by secretary Clarissa Saunders (Jean Arthur) and Senator Paine (Claude Rains), a revered elder statesman to Smith but another corrupt official to the party. Smith's naive, unworldly ways quickly make him a figure of fun to his Washington colleagues and the gentlemen of the press. However, he endears himself to Clarissa who develops into a staunch ally.

Smith's pet project is a bill to provide a camp for his Boy Rangers but the land is needed by the party and a smear campaign is begun which is so successful that Smith faces a vote on his expulsion from the House. With Clarissa's support he finds new strength and, encouraged by the Vice-President, he stages a marathon one-man filibuster. Hoarse of voice and worn to the point of exhaustion he refuses to bow to the pressures brought against him, vowing: 'You all think I'm licked. Well, I'm not licked and I'm going to stay right here and fight for this lost cause even if this room gets filled with lies like these . . . Somebody'll listen to me'. Somebody does: a conscience-stricken Senator Paine who tries to commit suicide but chooses the braver option of confessing the party's misdeeds and exonerating Smith.

Jefferson Smith provided Stewart with a physical and emotional tour-de-force, a role which crystallized his public appeal and set the parameters of his future screen image. His character develops from a naive, cock-eyed idealist, who reaches the depths of despair when shown the dirty reality of politics, and then finds the inner reserves to battle on because decency, honesty and integrity have to be worth defending regardless of the odds against the defender. In *Mr Smith* he emerges a shining beacon of virtue in a world of sham and cynicism.

The film went into production during the spring of 1939 with part of the filming on location in Washington and the Senate scenes completed on a studio recreation in Hollywood. Stewart's throat was treated twice a day to produce a swelling of his vocal chords and aid the authenticity of his filibuster scenes. Frank Capra told Peter Bogdanovich: 'When *Mr Smith* came along, it was either Cooper or Stewart, and Jim was younger an I knew he would make a hell of a Mr Smith — he looked like the country kid, the idealist — it was very close to him. I think there's no question but that this picture shaped the public image of him, of the real Jimmy Stewart'. Stewart concurs: 'Yeah, that was the picture . . . that was the first time I felt I was really getting across'.

Mr Smith Goes to Washington was one of the year's top box-office successes and it garnered for Stewart the first of five Best Actor Oscar nominations. His fellow nominees were Clark Gable (*Gone With the Wind*), Laurence Olivier (*Wuthering Heights*), Mickey Rooney (*Babes in Arms*) and, the winner, Robert Donat (*Goodbye, Mr Chips*). The film faced strong competition in many categories winning only one award—best original story for Lewis R.Foster, although Stewart did win the New York Critics Award for Best Male Performance. The film was released during the first months of the Second World War and *Mr Smith* was adopted as a universal symbol of the ordinary man and defender of right. In 1942 the film was chosen by theatres in occupied France as the final English-language film to be screened before the Nazi ban on American films was imposed.

Stewart's final release of 1939 was also to become a perennially popular classic: *Destry Rides Again*. His first western, directed by George Marshall and co-starring Marlene Dietrich, finds him as Tom Destry, mild-mannered man of peace, who believes that words speak louder than actions. In the Wild West of the 1870s his philosophy is little appreciated. Called to the town of Bottle Neck to act as deputy and help combat the local Mr Big, Kent (Brian Donlevy), Destry's initial appearance convinces the inhabitants that he is not to be taken seriously; he carries no guns and is holding a parasol and a canary for

'Destry' pours cold water on Marlene Dietrich and Una Merkel to stop their fight in Destry rides Again *(1939)*.

a fellow passenger. Destry however is made of sterner stuff and uses only his wit and intelligence to counter-act Kent's violence, until it is essential to strap on his six-shooters and prove that right is might. Along the way he encounters Dietrich's saloon singer Frenchy and appreciates the woman beneath the cheap facade. At the climax Frenchy sacrifices herself by stopping a bullet intended for Destry.

Tom Destry provided Stewart with an ideal follow-on to Mr Smith, the two characters are blood brothers who share common values and virtues as moralistic men and defenders of the good and the just. Destry is more worldly-wise and shrewd in his actions but he also helped contribute to the public's favourable impression of Stewart. Stewart's chemical reaction with Dietrich is also potent and the film did much to revive her career at a time when she had been labelled 'box-office poison'. Huskily singing 'See What the Boys in the Back Room Will Have' or 'Little Joe', and tearing into a raucous fight with Una Merkel, she successfully established a more down-to-earth image that replaced a previously aloof screen persona. The studio publicity hailed the film as 'The Greatest Feminine Fist Fight Ever Filmed' and Dietrich later commented, 'To think that after all these years it was a brawl and not a love scene that took me right to the top and kept me there!'

Stewart has often been accused of just playing Jimmy Stewart but in 1940 he showed the range of role of which he is capable; in four films he plays a Budapest shop assistant, an anti-Nazi farmer, a provincial playwright finding sudden acclaim in New York, and a scandal-sheet reporter with frustrated ambitions.

The Shop Around the Corner, a light and charming romance, vividly illustrates the reasons for the eminence of its director Ernst Lubitsch. Stewart is Alfred Kralik and Margaret Sullavan is Klara Novak, two quarrelsome co-workers in the leather goods and novelty store of Hugo Matuschek (Frank Morgan). Both carry on a romance with a penfriend known only as Dear Friend, each unaware that their postal partner is really the bothersome colleague at work. Over a busy Christmas season the truth is discovered and they accept the stronger feeling of their love over their unreasonable behaviour at the shop. The 'Lubitsch touch' invests this enterprise with a tenderness and grace that is built up in layers of small detail and delicately assured performances topped off with a dreamily perfect Budapest setting of the type that only ever existed on a Hollywood sound stage.

35

By comparison *The Mortal Storm* was a stark and dramatic anti-Nazi film that teamed Stewart and Sullavan for the fourth and final time as two lovers whose lives are touched and tarnished by the rise of Nazism. Stewart is Martin Breitner who becomes an increasingly isolated figure as his friends and peers are passionately involved in the ascendancy of Hitler, a movement Breitner views with alarm. One family to suffer immense hardship is the Roths when the Professor (Frank Morgan) is incarcerated in a concentration camp and later executed for being Jewish. Breitner has fled to Austria but returns to help rescue Freya Roth (Sullavan), the girl he loves. The couple are pursued across the mountains as they try to escape and Freya is shot dead by the storm troopers. Breitner carries her with him across the border.

It has often been said that the more human a character the better Stewart's acting is; in *The Mortal Storm* he is at his best facing ostracization from his friends, standing virtually alone in the face of fascism, risking all for love and knowing the anguish of loss. The film is an impressive indictment of Nazism and marked an unusually committed production from a country not yet at war with Germany.

No Time for Comedy, which followed, was a much more routine assignment. Stewart is Gaylord Esterbrook, a Minnesota journalist who writes a hit comedy, journeys to Broadway and marries the leading lady Linda (Rosalind Russell). They live happily ever after until Gaylord is smitten by a four-year itch in the shape of the alluring Amanda (Genevieve Tobin). He is convinced that he should be writing serious drama. The serious play is a tragedy in every sense and Gaylord happily returns to Linda. *No Time for Comedy* was no more than entertaining escapism but Stewart received his, by now, customarily fine notices; the New York *Times* observed: 'As usual, Mr Stewart is the best thing in the show — a completely ingratiating character who ranges from the charming clumsiness of a country playwright to the temperamental distraction of an established writer with complete and natural assurance.'

No Time for Comedy, a Warner Brothers film, had been based on a stage hit by S.N.Behrman which starred Katharine Cornell and Laurence Olivier. Stewart's next film, *The Philadelphia Story*, also had its roots on the stage.

In the late 1930s Katharine Hepburn found herself in a similar position to Stewart's *Destry* co-star Marlene Dietrich, that is, labelled 'box-office poison' and with a faltering career. Hepburn went to Broadway, scoring an immense personal triumph as a spoiled society girl Tracy Lord in Philip Barry's *The Philadelphia Story*. She would only return to Hollywood on her own terms, having shrewdly purchased the screen rights to her stage success. A package deal was struck with MGM. Hepburn received $250,000 and a one-picture contract for the film version of *The Philadelphia Story*. She requested Clark Gable and Spencer Tracy as her co-stars but was happy to settle for Cary Grant and James Stewart. Grant received top-billing and his choice of the two male roles as well as the stipulation that his salary be paid to British War Relief. He chose the part of the ex-husband, C.K.Dexter Haven, originated on the stage by Joseph Cotten, allowing Stewart to be cast as the reporter Macauley Connor, the part played in the theatre by Van Heflin. Hepburn's favourite director, George Cukor, was employed and the script was placed in the hands of Donald Ogden Stewart, a friend of the playwright. He later recalled, '*The Philadelphia Story* was such a good vehicle and Katharine had played it in New York. They had made a recording of it in the theatre with all the laughs, you see, and they'd play this and if I hadn't included a laugh that was in the play I'd have to go back and do it again — I was really writing against a tape recorder'.

The Philadelphia Story opens on the eve of Miss Tracy Lord's second marriage as events conspire to ensure that she doesn't arrive at the altar on time. Firstly, there is the arrival of two members of the journalistic profession employed by Spy magazine — Macauley, or Mike, Connor and photographer Liz Imbrie (Ruth Hussey). Then, Tracy's first husband returns to his old hunting ground.

The film's essence is the melting of an ice-cool, haughty, socially-prominent and single-minded woman as she is toppled from her lofty, well-guarded pedestal of reserve and arrogance. A tipsy midnight swim by Mike and Tracy is misconstrued by Tracy's fiancé who breaks off the engagement. Tracy has learnt the lesson of humility and realises that life with Dexter is really what she wants. A marriage goes ahead with Dexter and Tracy as groom and bride second time around.

The Philadelphia Story is a perfect example of a cocktail comedy of sophisticated humour and adult characters. The film opened at New York's Radio City Music Hall on Boxing Day of 1940 and ran for an unprecedented six weeks. In the major Oscar categories *The*

Philadelphia Story was nominated for best film, best director, best screenplay, best actress, best supporting actress (Hussey) and best actor for Stewart. The New York *Herald Tribune* summed up Stewart's importance to the film version even although he was the second male lead: 'Stewart, in the part of the snooping journalist who hates his job and wants to write real stuff, contributes most of the comedy to the show. His reaction to a snobbish society built on wealth is a delight to watch. In addition, he contributes some of the most irresistible romantic moments to the proceedings'.

The Oscars for 1940 were awarded on 27 February, 1941 in a ceremony with Bob Hope as host. The event was a special occasion as Franklin Roosevelt became the first American President to address the Academy. He declared, 'The American motion picture as a national and an international force is a phenomenon of our own generation. Within living memory we have seen it born and grow up into full maturity. We have seen the American motion picture become foremost in the world. We have seen it reflect our civilisation throughout the rest of the world — the aims and aspirations and ideals of a free people and of freedom.' The prestigious husband and wife team of Alfred Lunt and Lynne Fontanne were on hand to present the Best Actress and Best Actor Awards to Ginger Rogers for *Kitty Foyle* and to James Stewart. Stewart had faced competition from Charles Chaplin (*The Great Dictator*), Henry Fonda (*The Grapes of Wrath*), Raymond Massey (*Abe Lincoln in Illinois*) and Laurence Olivier (*Rebecca*). Years later Stewart revealed that he had voted for his good friend Fonda adding, 'Of course I also voted for Alfred Landon, Wendell Wilkie and Thomas E.Dewey'. There was some feeling that his Oscar might have been a consolation prize for losing the previous year and Stewart has said, 'I never thought that much of my work in *The Philadelphia Story*'. Stewart gave his Oscar to his father who put it on display in his hardware store. 'First it was on the knife counter, then he put a cheese bell over it . . Goodness knows why! Then he put it in the front window where it stayed for twenty years. Now it's at home in my library.'

The Philadelphia Story and the Academy Award marked a professional high-water mark for James Stewart, but the trio of films he made afterwards was a distinct anti-climax. In *Come Live With Me*, a comedy, he is a penniless author who marries Hedy Lamarr and thus saves her from deportation. *Pot O'Gold* was produced by James

Stewart gained an Oscar for The Philadelphia Story *but 'never thought much of his work in it'*.

Roosevelt, the President's son, and found Stewart as a harmonica player who helps a band of struggling musicians to radio fame and fortune; while he was one of many stars in MGM's *Ziegfeld Girl* as Lana Turner's long-suffering boy-friend. Hardly an inspiring trio of roles for the man chosen as the Best Actor of 1940 ahead of Chaplin and Olivier. MGM had promised him a starring role in *Wings on His Back* but by then the actor had decided to go to war.

Stewart had bought a yellow two-seater Stimson 105 plane and had built up his flying time so that he had over four hundred hours in the air to offer as experience. On the first attempt to enlist he was rejected for being ten pounds too light for his height, much to the relief of the MGM studio executives who resented his insistence on serving in the forces. A high calorie diet, and Stewart's stubbornness, saw him accepted as a private in the US Army Air Force on 22 March, 1941. He was the first major film star to enlist and he insisted on the minimum of fuss. Accepting a salary cut from $12,000 a month to $21 he set off for active service with a MGM farewell committee at the railway station that included Jeanette MacDonald, Clarke Gable, Myrna Loy, and Louis B. Mayer himself.

Chapter 4

Stewart served six months as an aircraft mechanic and was then commissioned as a Second Lieutenant instructing cadets. He rose to the rank of Lieutenant-Colonel, was based in Britain with the Eighth Air Force B-24 Squadron, and flew some twenty-five missions over enemy territory. His bomber was named 'Nine Yanks and a Jerk'. He returned to America in September 1945 as Colonel James Stewart, the recipient of the Air Medal, Distinguished Flying Cross with Oak Leaf Cluster, the Croix de Guerre with Palm, and seven battle stars. For many years after the war, he remained active in the Air Force Reserve, becoming a Brigadier-General. Stewart has always been fairly reticent in discussing his wartime experiences but 'I value my connection with the military above all else,' he said. 'Of course, I love the glamour of making movies. Of course, I love being well-known and highly paid. But those years flying combat missions somehow made my life seem worthwhile'.

During the war Stewart had found an opportunity to recreate his *Philadelphia Story* role on radio with Grant and Hepburn in a Victory Show for the Government broadcast on 20 July, 1942. He had also appeared at the Oscar ceremony on 26 Feberary, 1942 to present the Best Actor Oscar to his good friend Gary Cooper for his role in *Sergeant York*. Even so, when he resumed his film career in April of 1946 it had been five years since he last stepped in front of the cameras. The war had obviously changed him and he seriously doubted the wisdom of remaining in the comparatively frivolous profession of acting: 'I've often thought about what it (the war) did,' he said. 'I don't know really. People say, "You matured". Well, you're supposed to . . . you're five years older . . . you're supposed to be more mature. Being away that long, having the experience that I had . . I have a feeling that it was to my advantage as an actor, but I don't know how to go much further than that.'

His contract with MGM expired during the war and, thanks to pioneering legal advances, the studio was unable to force him to serve out the years of his absence. He chose not to renew with the studio, deciding to freelance instead, and he selected his first role from an idea by Frank Capra for Liberty Films. The actor made one stipulation before signing his contract: in any publicity for the film there was to be no 'Mention or cause to be mentioned the part taken by his participation as an officer in the USAAF'. The clause was agreed and the film went into production; it was to be called *It's A Wonderful Life*.

In 1939 Philip Van Doren Stern's short story *The Greatest Gift* had been sent to his friends as a Christmas card and was subsequently published. RKO bought the rights to the story, planning to make a film with Cary Grant. Frank Capra purchased the rights from RKO and began developing the script of *It's A Wonderful Life*. Stewart plays George Bailey, a citizen of the small town of Bedford Falls. As a young man he has dreams of travelling the world and carving out a successful career as an architect. However, he is called upon to make many sacrifices, relinquishing his hopes and aspirations along the way as he takes over the family business of Bailey Building and Loans, eking out a living with his loving wife Mary (Donna Reed) and four children. One Christmas he faces financial ruin and public scandal when his bumbling Uncle Billie (Thomas Mitchell) loses $8,000 of the company money. All his pent-up frustrations and bitterness rise to the surface as he squares up to a moment of bleak despair. Contemplating suicide he cries out: 'I wish I'd never been born'. At this stage Clarence (Henry Travers), an angel, is sent to present George with a vision of his hometown bereft of his life — his wife is a spinster working in the library, his brother dies as a child because George wasn't there to save him, his mother runs a boarding house, his friends are consigned to slums and the town is named Pottersville after the local, avaricious businessman and slum landlord. Shocked by these visions George is happy to return to his lot, aware that a man's wealth is measured by his friends and the way he

Stewart's return to film-making after the Second World War was in Frank Capra's It's a Wonderful Life, *with Donna Reed, Thomas Mitchell (left) and Beulah Bondi (right).*

touches the lives of others. Friends rally around to provide the missing $8,000 and everyone can enjoy a Happy Christmas, including Clarence who, as an angel, has won his wings.

Capra's Christmas story is a tale of Dickensian proportions with Lionel Barrymore's Potter the equivalent of Scrooge and the moral, of salvation in friendship, generosity and community, skating on similar territory. Stewart is called upon to portray a complex set of emotions as the small-town dreamer continually forced to bow before harsh reality. The film provides numerous magical moments — Stewart and Reed dancing the Charleston and winding up in the college pool, Stewart falling in love with Reed during a shared phone-call, a hollow-eyed, unshaven Stewart gripped by panic, and a final image of family and friends joined in joyous Christmas celebration. Both Stewart and Capra regard the film as their favourite from amongst all their work. Stewart had questioned his further career in acting, but a firm lecture from Lionel Barrymore and the quality of his experience on *It's A Wonderful Life* convinced him where his future lay. The film received five Academy Award nominations including Best Actor for Stewart. The film, Capra's masterpiece, went empty-handed on the night and was also a modest failure at the box-office showing a deficit of $525,000. It appeared that, times having changed, the public appetite for Capra 'corn' had abated.

Stewart moved on to *Magic Town*, a sub-Capra piece written and produced by Robert Riskin, a frequent collaborator of Capra's. Stewart plays a pollster, Laurence 'Rip' Smith, who discovers a perfectly average American town whose unconscious averageness is ruined by his exploitation. Full of remorse for his actions, and in love with the editor of the local newspaper, Mary Peterman (Jane Wyman), he redeems himself and restores the self-esteem of the towns-people. The film is pleasant and humorous in a satirical vein but found little public favour. The director William Wellman offered a harsh criticism when he stated, 'It stunk! If you think *Magic Town* has anything good about it at all there's something wrong with you'.

During the summer of 1947 Stewart returned to Broadway, acting as a seven-week summer replacement for Frank Fay in Mary Chase's hit play *Harvey*. Stewart had seen Fay in the role and recalled, 'In the interval Brock Pemberton, producer of the comedy, saw me in the bar and, when I told him how much I was loving the show, suggested that if I wanted to take a rest from Hollywood movies for a short while why didn't I take over from Frank Fay for a few weeks? I couldn't wait to say yes and that's how I started what seems to have been a career in itself'. Stewart enjoyed his return to the boards and came back, by request, the following spring.

Stewart's film career went now through a busy and problematic phase as he sought an image in keeping with his values and the mood of post-war audiences. *Call Northside 777* was one of a popular school of film-making in the late 1940s — the semi-documentary, realist drama. Henry Hathaway directed a diligent Stewart as the dogged reporter P.J.McNeal who uncovers evidence that leads to the release of a man falsely accused of murder. Filmed largely on locations in Chicago the film was based on a true incident involving a journalist on the *Chicago Times*, James P.McGuire, who acted as adviser to the production.

Stewart's two comedy roles in 1948 productions were less successful. *You Gotta Stay Happy* starred Joan Fontaine and was produced by her husband William Dozier. A throwback to the screwball comedies of a decade earlier the film finds Fontaine as a runaway bride and heiress with Stewart comfortably cast as a pilot. *Time* magazine declared: 'This is the kind of role that Stewart could play blindfolded, hog-tied and in the bottom of a well'. Audiences may have thought so too and they decided to stay away. Nor did they turn up in large numbers for *On Our Merry Way* in one episode of which Stewart and Henry Fonda enact a John O'Hara story. Alfred Hitchcock's *Rope* came under the heading of an 'interesting experiment' as the great director attempted a film using the ten-minute take to create an apparently seamless, continuous story. The process put a great technical challenge to the actors as their co-ordination with roving cameras and mikes became even more crucial to a film where the camera cannot just cut to someone else's reaction or point of view. Based on the play by Patrick Hamilton, *Rope* tells of two students, Brandon (John Dall) and Philip (Farley Granger), who murder a friend for the sheer thrill of it and to enact the philosophies of their teacher Rupert Cadell (Stewart) on 'superior men' who are above the law. They hold a dinner party with food served on an old chest containing the body, but from their manner and the absence of the deceased Cadell realises their crime. He is shocked by the seemingly logical extreme to which his views have been extended.

James Stewart and family, 1951.

Rope is a blackly comic diversion on the ethics of murder with Stewart miscast as the older, donnish academic, a pivotal role in which he found much humour. However, he did appreciate working with Hitchcock and earned $300,000 for his role.

Stewart was seen in two 1949 releases; the later one was *Malaya*, originally entitled 'Operation Malaya'. Set during the war as the Allies attempt to smuggle rubber supplies the film is routine action fare and a disservice to a strong cast led by Spencer Tracy and Stewart, who is killed before the film's climax. More important was *The Stratton Story*, a fondly remembered biography of the baseball player Monty Stratton who triumphed over the loss of one leg to resume his career. Stewart is called upon to portray an all-American hero, facing tragedy, who endures through an unquenchable spirit and the love of his wife (June Allyson) and friends. It was an ideal role and a popular film, in America at least, where it was the number six box-office attraction of 1949 taking almost $4 million. It also proved that, if the prime Stewart characteristics were properly utilised, where audience identification was high, then he was as potent a performer as ever. The New York *Times* wrote, '*The Stratton Story* is the best thing that has yet happened to Mr Stewart in his post-war film career . . . Mr Stewart gives such a winning performance that it is almost impossible to imagine anyone else playing the role'.

Off-screen the best thing to happen to Stewart was his marriage to Gloria Hatrick McLean on 9 August, 1949. A former model, divorced and with two children, Ronald and Michael, Gloria, ten years Stewart's junior, met the actor at a dinner party given by the Gary Coopers in 1947. Over the years Stewart's name had been linked with Ginger Rogers, Olivia De Havilland, Rita Hayworth and many others. He believed, 'When you're forty-one, life means more than just a bookful of phone numbers. I needed the security of a permanent relationship with a woman I loved. I needed a family and I needed to put down roots. I can say all the usual things about meeting the right girl and falling in love. But it was also the right time'. So much so that the couple are still together over thirty-five years later.

Chapter 5

Stewart's career has followed a very steady course, rarely displaying signs of faltering popularity or the often alarming peaks and throughs more characteristic of those who endure. Yet, he was clearly encountering difficulties in finding his feet in the post-war film world. His outstanding film, *It's A Wonderful Life*, had been a box-office failure and it seemed that audience requirements were changing in a way that might have left Stewart high and dry.

At the time Stewart was wise enough to acknowledge the problem as he later told Peter Bogdanovich: 'I realised after the war that I wasn't going across any more — after a couple of pictures. I remember on *Magic Town*, one critic wrote, 'If we have to sit through another picture while that beanpole stumbles around, taking forever to get things out'. The New York *Times* sent a guy out here to do an article on me, and he said, "Now, I'll tell you right off, the title of this thing is gonna be The Rise and Fall of Jimmy Stewart!" I realised I'd better do something — I couldn't just go on hemming and hawing — which I'd sometimes overdid too . . . I looked at an old picture of mine — *Born to Dance* — I wanted to vawmit! I had t'. .toughen it up. .I gawt. . tougher—and I found that in Westerns I could do it an' still retain what I was. People would accept it.'

Of course Stewart had previously made a Western, *Destry Rides Again*, but that had been partly comic in tone. Throughout the 1950s, particularly in his films with Anthony Mann, Stewart built up an image of a tough, resourceful Westerner with a stubborn streak often driven onwards by revenge or passion. He was no slouch in the

47

horse-riding stakes either; 'My dad always had a horse in back of the hardware store. I guess I shovelled manure more than I learned how to ride but I learned to be around horses y'know. So this was a great asset when I started doing Westerns.' The first of these was *Broken Arrow*, from Elliot Arnold's historical novel *Blood Brother*, and it was filmed entirely on location in northern Arizona. Released in 1950 it painted the Apache nation in a comparatively sympathetic manner, something of a rarity for the time. Stewart is a Civil War veteran, Tom Jeffords, who learns the language and customs of the Apache in an attempt to meet with Cochise (Jeff Chandler) and facilitate a truce between the white man and the redskin. Jeffords marries an Indian girl Sonseeahry (Debra Paget) and peace is secured but at the cost of the girl's life.

Broken Arrow is an earnest, well-intentioned drama written in the atmosphere of the 'Cold War'. Time, however, has exposed its simplistic, even sentimental view of the Apache. The love affair between sixteen year-old Paget and forty-one year-old Stewart is not the most convincing. Surprisingly, several contemporary reviewers expressed unease at the presence of Stewart in a Western. The New York *Times* was especially severe observing, 'Mr Stewart is a human specimen of miserable account. He fumbles his words, waves his hands in lazy gestures and throws his whole enterprise on a casual plane'. The *Saturday Review* added; "Jeff Chandler. .steals the picture away from Jimmy who always seems on the verge of saying to the cameramen, 'Aw gee, fellows, let's go back and play baseball'." It was hardly the most auspicious start for a career Out West. However, everything else that happened to Stewart in 1950 was touched by success.

No longer under contract to a studio Stewart became a pioneer in the freelance stakes, one of the first major stars of the modern era to forego a fixed salary in exchange for a sizeable share of the profits. It was a policy that would make him one of the wealthiest men in Hollywood. Universal was particularly happy to work the financial side of an actor's participation in this way. Abbott and Costello had enjoyed a similar arrangement with the company and thus Stewart was involved in a package deal at Universal that included the film version of *Harvey* and a property called *Winchester '73*. Stewart has made light of his business acumen in acquiring a large profit percentage of his films: 'The truth is that I'm a very poor mathematician. I

Broken Arrow *(1950)*, *a 'pro Indian' Western.*

Harvey *(1950)*, *his own favourite part.*

kept flunking algebra although I could do something called descriptive geometry. I've never been very close to the financial part of the picture business but when it was sugested to me, it seemed a logical and sensible way of looking at it. You were much more part of the picture because you had more at stake in the outcome'.

Winchester '73 is as significant a landmark in the formation of Stewart's post-war image as *Mr Smith* had been to his pre-war one. The film uses an episodic format to relay the adventures of a group of people whose common characteristic is their fleeting possession of a Winchester '73 repeating rifle. The heart of the matter is the quest by one man, Lin McAdam (Stewart), and his partner High Spade (Millard Mitchell), to avenge the death of his father at the hands of Dutch Henry Brown (Stephen McNally). As the rifle passes from a trader to an Indian and others, on its circuitous route from McAdam to Brown, the former continues his relentness pursuit of his quarry. In a gun battle in the mountains McAdam kills Brown who has only recently been revealed to the audience as McAdam's brother.

Stewart's character in *Winchester '73* is tougher; Lin McAdam is a man hardened in the saddle by a bitter hatred for his father's killer, capable of vicious action when his patience frays as the final showdown nears. The earlier Stewart characteristics of hesitancy and a diffident fumbling are restrained and checked by his conscious decision to allow more maturity in his performance. On the film's release it was an immediate and huge success. 'You might call it a desperation move,' Stewart has said. 'I found that I was relying on the sort of romantic comedy style I had helped develop before the war. I'd sort of fallen back on it. But it wasn't accepted. The public seemed to want either the wild, slapstick type of comedy or pretty serious stuff like war stories.'

The fickle public taste in comedy was reflected in the disappointing box-office returns for *Harvey*. Stewart repeated his stage work as Elwood P.Dowd, a middle-aged dreamer who has created an invisible white rabbit, Harvey, who serves as his best friend and means of coping with life. Unfortunately Dowd's sister Veta (Josephine Hull) sees Harvey as a sign of Elwood's failing grip on sanity and is extremely worried when she too begins to see Harvey. After an attempt to have Elwood institutionalised Veta accepts the value of Harvey to her brother and is content to tolerate his special 'friend'.

The persona of Elwood P. Dowd, a gentle, benevolent soul, gave

Stewart one of his most fondly remembered roles. Mooning around, happily inhabiting his own world of goodwill Stewart's Dowd is a figure of some considerable pathos. He received his fourth Academy Award nomination as Best Actor facing competition from Louis Calhern (*The Magnificent Yankee*), William Holden (*Sunset Boulevard*), Spencer Tracy (*Father of the Bride*) and, the winner, José Ferrer (*Cyrano de Bergerac*). Josephine Hull, however, won the best supporting actress award, *Harvey's* only Oscar.

Stewart's final release of 1950 was *The Jackpot*, an amiable domestic comedy. The script was based on the true story of Jim Caffrey of Wakefield, Rhode Island, who had correctly named Louis B.Mayer as the 'mystery voice' on the 'Sing It Again' show and won $24,000 in prizes that cost him more than their value. In the film Stewart plays Bill Lawrence whose initial joy at scooping the jackpot on 'Name the Mystery Husband' turns to consternation when faced with a huge income-tax bill and the problem of what to do with the prizes that include 7,500 cans of soup, a Shetland pony and 12 wrist watches. His domestic harmony is totally disrupted and his wife is jealous of the beautiful artist who comes to paint his picture — another prize. Only after a trying time is harmony restored.

Stewart was on view in only one new film in 1951, Nevil Shute's *No Highway* (known in America as *No Highway in the Sky*). It had been filmed in Britain during the autumn of the previous year. Stewart plays an absent-minded boffin Theodore Honey, an engineer with the Royal Aircraft Establishment. His firm belief in the inadequacy of the tail assembly of a new aircraft, the Reindeer, is considered eccentric. He is certain that metal fatigue will cause the tail assembly to snap after 1,440 flying hours. A chance to test his theory arises when he boards a Reindeer flight to Labrador. He tries to convince the other passengers of the impending peril. During a stop-over in Gander the plane is passed as airworthy despite Honey's protests. When Honey wrecks the undercarriage to prevent the continuation of the flight he is considered insane. Two travelling companions, stewardess Marjorie Corder (Glynis Johns) and film star Monica Teasdale (Marlene Dietrich), have been won over by his conviction and help to clear his name. He is vindicated when his theory is proved to have been true.

Stewart's absent-minded professor in *No Highway* was well within his previously accepted range and, alongside *The Jackpot*, marked a temporary farewell to comic characterisations. The film allows for a disappointing reunion with his *Destry* co-star whose role here adds an element of incidental glamour but lacks the bite and impact of their previous meeting. A solid example of screen entertainment *No Highway* was modestly successful and one can speculate that its appeal for Stewart might have resided in the subject-matter (flying) and the chance to film in Britain.

The new 'image' of a man of the West had struck a strong chord with the public and, when the list of major box-office stars for 1950 was published, Stewart made his first appearance in the all-important top ten. He was reckoned to be the fifth top box-office attraction after John Wayne, Bob Hope, Bing Crosby and Betty Grable. Apart from 1951 he would stay in the 'top ten' throughout the entire decade, many of his films proving to be among the most popular of their year and his decision to work for a profit percentage looked more and more like the best financial move of his career.

Privately, 1951 was a year of family happiness for Stewart when twin daughters, Judy and Kelly, were born on 7 May, 1951. In his 1966 interview with Peter Bogdanovich Stewart bubbled over with paternal joy; 'And the twins . . I think now that if they have pills to stawp babies: they ougtha be able to have pills that make *twins*! Because . . I think it's . . the most wonderful . . They're never lonely . . they're . . and they have a bond between them that's . . They . . they hold secret meetings in the cellar . . and I can't go . . no-one's allowed down there—no-one . . but the dog!'

The half-a-dozen years since the war had seen major changes in Stewart's life and career; his bachelor days were over and he was now a happily married family man, father and provider to four children; after a hiccough in his screen fortunes he had emerged with a more mature range of characteristics that would enhance his basic popularity; and, finally, he had dispelled any doubts of his own over the merits of acting as a profession. As if to prove the latter point he was working at a concerted pace with three films on release each year in 1952 and 1953.

Cecil B.DeMille's *The Greatest Show on Earth* is a lavish and garish three-ring circus of show-business clichés. It was also the most popular film released in America during 1953, taking some $14 million at the box-office, and was chosen the best film of the year at the Academy Awards in the face of competition from *High Noon*,

Ivanhoe, Moulin Rouge and *The Quiet Man.* In terms of Stewart's career it was a handy film in which to be seen. The idea for a circus film first came to DeMille in 1949 and he spent a substantial amount of time researching the authentic flavour of the Big Top, travelling extensively with the Ringling Brothers. Intent on creating an extravaganza of epic proportions De Mille wanted to people his cast with star names; Burt Lancaster, Kirk Douglas, Marlene Dietrich and Hedy Lamarr were all considered at some stage. Eventually the line-up included Charlton Heston, Cornel Wilde, Betty Hutton, Gloria Grahame and Stewart in a piece of enjoyable hokum and sawdust life and rivalries which culminates in a spectacular train crash and a plucky troop intent on proving that the show must go on. Stewart's role is of modest size but makes a telling extended cameo as sad-faced clown Buttons whose make-up masks his identity: a doctor wanted for the mercy-killing of his wife.

In the next film, *Bend of the River* Stewart is back in the saddle under the firm directorial reins of Anthony Mann. Here Stewart is Glyn McLyntock, once a Missouri border raider, now reformed. Acting as a guide for a group of fruit farmers headed for Oregon he is partnered by a horse thief, Emerson Cole (Arthur Kennedy), whom he has rescued from a lynching mob. When a settlement is built McLyntock is entrusted to bring supplies back to the farmers from Portland. When he arrives in Portland he finds it an overnight boomtown, transformed by a gold rush, and that the farmers' supplies have taken on a value beyond mere money. Cole quickly reverts to villainy, as the lure of wealth exerts its hold, and clashes with McLyntock who has assumed the role of defender of the farmers. The two men fight and McLyntock drowns Cole and saves the day for his friends.

Bend of the River is a typical example of the modest excellence of the Stewart-Mann collaboration, utilising the mountains and rivers of Oregon as a natural backdrop to a sparely created Western. Stewart's character is a flawed hero intent on proving the redeemable good in all and having to suffer intensively for this cause. Ragged and beaten, he vows to Arthur Kennedy's Cole, 'You'll be seeing me'. The strength of Kennedy's sneeringly charming villainy is again a feature of the Mann Westerns, representing the hero's alter ego and the thin line dividing the good and the bad.

Stewart's all-American values have often been called upon to

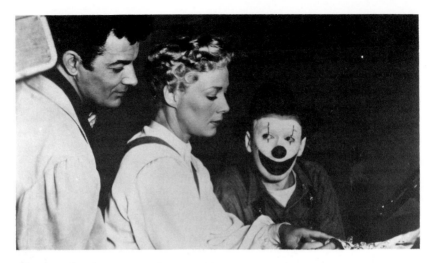

Wearing a clown's mask in Cecil B.De Mille's The Greatest Show on Earth *(1952), with Betty Hutton and Cornel Wilde.*

The modest excellence of the collaboration between Stewart and director Anthony Mann is shown by Bend of the River, *with Arthur Kennedy who also appeared in* The Man from Laramie *(opposite) where Stewart is seen handing over his gun to the sherriff (see pages 63–4).*

portray the real characters of his country's history. His final 1952 release, *Carbine Williams*, was one such venture but one of the actor's least successful vehicles. Stewart is Marsh Williams, an illegal moonshiner in prohibition North Carolina who receives a thirty-year prison sentence on a charge of second degree murder following a run-in with Revenue agents. Whilst incarcerated he invents a 30 M-I carbine rifle which sees extensive service during the Second World War. For his contribution to the war effort, Williams is pardoned.

By all accounts Williams was a sullen and selfish rebel who reacted bitterly to the discipline forced upon him by prison life, hardly an ideal role for the Stewart persona. However, *Bend of the River* was one of the year's hit films and, combined with *The Greatest Show on Earth*, placed Stewart at position six in the list of box-office stars behind Bob Hope, Bing Crosby, John Wayne, Gary Cooper and, top favourites, Dean Martin and Jerry Lewis.

The fruitful relationship with Anthony Mann continued in 1953 with the director responsible for all three of Stewart's releases. *The Naked Spur* is a further stark refinement of the basic elements in their Western partnership. Stewart is Howard Kemp, a lone figure in pursuit of escaped killer Ben Vandergroat (Robert Ryan) who has a $5,000 price on his head, dead or alive. Along the way others are involved in the capture of Vandergroat and his companion Lina (Janet Leigh). Tensions develop among the group, resulting in several deaths and the climactic union of Lina and Howard. *The Naked Spur* is an elemental tale built around the basest of human emotions — greed and lust. Stewart's opportunist bounty-hunter is only marginally less self-seeking than the other characters but again proves capable of redemption through the love of a woman who cares.

Thunder Bay is a disappointment, showing Stewart and Mann failing by their own, admittedly high, standards. A tale of tension amidst oilmen and shrimp fishermen in the waters of Port Felicity, Louisiana the film is an ordinary story, rather too patly resolved by the simultaneous discovery of oil and a shrimp bed. However, *The Glenn Miller Story*, which followed, is an altogether different venture.

A warmly engaging and nostalgic biography of the popular American bandleader, *The Glenn Miller Story* features a faithful, well-modulated impersonation of Miller by Stewart. Like the Mann Westerns the film chronicles a kind of adventure as the musician and

Perhaps his most famous and popular role, as Glenn Miller (1953).

his wife Helen (June Allyson) sacrifice all in their quest to find 'the sound' that will so distinguish the music of Glenn Miller. Stewart is at ease with the musical demands the role places upon him as he simulated trombone-playing to the genuine sounds of Joe Yuki. He had made a special request for June Allyson as his co-star and there is a relaxed confidence and easy warmth in their screen relationship. Even if it is a sentimental show-business story, orchestrated by Henry Mancini and glowingly photographed by William Daniels, the film was deservedly a massive popular hit.

Stewart was the 'number seven' box-office star in 1953 and it was said that, as a freelance, he could now demand and expect a deal that allowed him 50% of a film's profits. As, on its general release in 1954, *The Glenn Miller Story* grossed around $7 million dollars, and was re-issued in 1960, one estimate of his profit participation reckoned that Stewart earned more than one million dollars from that film.

Chapter 6

Stewart was now enjoying some of the best years of his screen life. Over the next four years, he was to make three films with Alfred Hitchcock, one of his favourite directors. The first, *Rear Window*, co-starred Grace Kelly, possibly his favourite leading lady.

Stewart liked working with 'Hitch' because of his ability as a story-teller: 'He is a very visual person. An old-school fellow. He feels that if you can't tell a story visually without a lot of dialogue, you are not using the film medium properly.' By hiring Stewart Hitchcock not only acquired the services of a fine actor but also gained a box-office asset. It was estimated that Stewart's name could now add an extra million dollars to a film's revenue because of his popularity in the all-important mid-west of America. Hitchcock once offered an analysis of Stewart as 'the perfect Hitchcock hero'. 'The enormous advantage in casting the star is because of familiarity,' he said. 'You see, the moment he gets into jeopardy the audience reaction is much stronger than it would be if the actor were a character man, who might be more right for the part. So your story is helped enormously. He is Everyman in bizarre situations. I mean, let's look at his private life — Princeton, Air Force Colonel — he's not an uneducated oaf, you can believe him as a professor, a doctor, family man.'

Shot on one claustrophobic sound-stage *Rear Window* casts Stewart as a photographer, L.B.'Jeff' Jeffries. Confined to his Manhattan apartment with his leg in plaster, he combats the boredom and frustration by taking an insatiable interest in the lives of his neighbours. From his window he spies on romantic newlyweds, a

59

'*The perfect Hitchcock hero*'; *James Stewart in* Rear Window *with Grace Kelly; with Doris Day in* The Man Who Knew Too Much; *and with Kim Novak in* Vertigo, *and on his own, high up, in the same film.*

61

lonely spinster, a voluptuous blonde carrying out her daily exercises, and then he faces his dawning awareness that the man opposite has murdered his wife. Jeff's society girl-friend Lisa (Grace Kelly), and his policeman friend Doyle (Wendell Corey), are convinced that his confinement has led to an over-active imagination. Jeff convinces Lisa of his suspicions and she risks her life seeking corroborating evidence whilst he faces the killer (Raymond Burr) alone in the apartment. The police arrive in time but not before Jeff plunges from his window ledge breaking his other leg.

Rear Window is a superbly crafted piece of cinema which works as both a tense thriller as well as providing a sub-text on voyeurism, eroticism and the art of film-acting itself. Although restricted to a wheelchair Stewart shows what real film-acting is in his ability subtly to convey reactions to each nuance of behaviour and twist of plot, while Grace Kelly brings a strong sexual charge to her role as the ice-cool blonde in search of love and a murderer in the steamy New York summer.

Rear Window was only slightly behind *The Glenn Miller Story* in the 1954 list of top money-makers and Stewart was the 'number four' box-office star in America. Thirty years on, *Rear Window* showed in its revival that it remains a thriller of wit and invention that amply demonstrates why Hitchcock is still regarded as a 'Master of Suspense'.

Before reuniting with Hitchcock Stewart returned to the capable hands of Anthony Mann and a trio of films, two Westerns and an aerial drama.

The Far Country was filmed in Canada during the summer of 1953 but went unreleased until the spring of 1955. Stewart's character, Jeff Webster, is an obstinate loner who looks after number one. He shares a dream with his partner, Ben Tatum (Walter Bennan), that one day they will own a ranch in Utah. To finance their plan they intend to sell their herd in Skagway, Alaska. However, the two men fall foul of the local law and, in the course of their struggle, Ben is killed as is Ronda Castle (Ruth Roman), a saloon-singer who has aided Jeff. By the time Jeff revenges their deaths his outlook has changed and he realises the true value of friends, of helping each other, and of community. As with the earlier Mann Westerns Stewart is a flawed hero, displaying many unpleasant characteristics; he is selfish, stubborn in his self-reliance and callous in his disregard for his fellow men. These frayed edges make his final redemption all the more telling.

Strategic Air Command, the second of the 1955 Mann trio, is an embarrassingly uncritical, flag-waving exercise in publicity for the peacetime American Air Force. Stewart plays Lieutenant-Colonel Holland who is called up from a lucrative baseball career to aid the development of long-range bombers in the post-war era. His initial resentment, and his feeling that he has already done more than his fair share for his country, are soon put aside as he responds to the greater calls of duty and patriotism. Eventually he signs-on as a professional. June Allyson portrays Stewart's screen wife for the third time and is there to fulfil the requirements of the traditional role of tolerant wife, mother and sidelines worrier. To a long-standing Republican and solid US citizen the film must have appealed as a vehicle expressing a viewpoint close to the actor's own. He believed that his service years endowed him with 'principles and standards (that) made me a better civilian'. Whatever its lack of dramatic merit *Strategic Air Command* certainly found favour with the great mass of American moviegoers, grossing in excess of $6½ million.

The Man from Laramie, however, represents the apotheosis of the Stewart-Mann actor-director partnership. Mann once said, 'I wanted to recapitulate, somehow, my five years of collaboration with Jimmy Stewart; that piece distilled our relationship. I reprised themes and situations by pushing them to their paroxysms'. A taut and brutal Western, *The Man from Laramie* finds Stewart as cowboy Will Lockhart who seeks revenge on those responsible for the death of his younger brother, a cavalry officer killed by Apaches armed with automatic rifles. In the town of Coronado in New Mexico he encounters the empire of Alec Waggoman (Donald Crisp) and is bush-wacked by his sadistic son Dave (Alex Nicol). Waggoman recompenses him for damages but orders Will to leave town. Will stays, finding a tentative romance with Waggoman's niece Barbara (Cathy O'Donnell). Later he is framed for two murders, including Dave's, but uncovers the real culprit, Waggoman's ranch foreman Vic (Arthur Kennedy) who was also largely responsible for selling the rifles to the Apaches who killed his brother. At a critical moment, when Will has cornered Vic and is savouring his imminent revenge, the two men are subject to an Indian attack and are forced to join forces for mutual survival. In the aftermath Will is unable to kill Vic and allows him to live.

In *The Man from Laramie* Stewart's character spends 104 minutes exorcising his own personal demons, and Stewart the actor suffers tremendous physical hardship to bring an intensity of conviction to his role. He burns with seething indignation as he faces a bullet shot into his hand or is dragged along the ground through dirt and fire. Strikingly shot in CinemaScope the film proved an excellent summation of the Mann-Stewart theme of obsession leading to moral redemption. It was their final film together and remains Stewart's favourite Western.

At the close of 1955 Stewart was named the top box-office attraction in USA. Around this time he was announced for several projects, including *Jewel of Bengal* opposite Jane Russell, and *Designing Woman* with Joshua Logan and Grace Kelly as his intended director and co-star. He later expressed regret at not having made the latter project. 'It was a very well-written property, produced by MGM, and we had the costumes all ready, and the sets were all built and everything,' he recalled in 1983. 'Then Grace Kelly came to see Mr Mayer, and said, "Mr Mayer I'm going to get married". And he said, "Well, that's just fine". "No," she said, "you don't understand." So she then told him the whole story — who she was to marry. So that was that. Monaco got a wonderful, wonderful Princess, but the movies lost a wonderful, wonderful, wonder girl.

'When they said, well, we'll get someone else, I said, 'I don't know — this was just right for Grace, and I don't think I want to do it without her. Well, I was completely wrong. I wish now I had done it. Betty Bacall did it and she was wonderful, and Greg Peck did my part, and it was a very successful movie.'

If Stewart was unable to work further with Grace Kelly there were no impediments to a reunion with Hitchcock, who quickly assembled a remake of his 1934 film *The Man Who Knew Too Much* especially for the actor. The film was to be made on locations in Britain and Morocco, with Doris Day as leading lady. American surgeon Ben McKenna (Stewart) is on holiday in Marrakech with his wife Jo (Day) and son Hank (Christopher Olsen). The family becomes inadvertently involved in international intrigue when Ben is passed a message by a dying French secret service agent informing him of an assassination plot. Young Hank is kidnapped by the plotters to ensure the silence of the McKennas. The couple travel on to London where Ben begins his own enquiries to rescue Hank from the clutches of the seemingly benign English couple Mr and Mrs Drayton (Bernard Miles and Brenda de Banzie). The chase takes him to the Albert Hall and a performance by the London Symphony Orchestra where a visiting prime minister is to be shot just as the cymbals clash. Ben and Jo race against the clock both to prevent the assassination and free their son.

Seen today *The Man Who Knew Too Much* is the weakest of the Stewart-Hitchcock films. It is Hitchcock's most obvious casting of the actor as the outraged paterfamilias; a far less interesting role than either of those in *Rear Window* or *Vertigo*. Nor was the 1934 plot sophisticated enough for 1956. Nevertheless the film was popular and allowed Doris Day to introduce the song Que Sera, Sera. It also gave a further illustration of Hitchcock's visual sense of film-making as Stewart has recounted; 'Doris and I had a long scene in the Albert Hall. The scene took place in the back of the hall with the London Symphony Orchestra on stage performing a symphony. While the orchestra played, Doris and I had dialogue to explain what was happening and what might happen afterwards. In the midst of the scene, Hitchcock appeared and said to us, "You two are talking so much I can't enjoy the symphony. Cut all the dialogue and act out the scene." Doris thought he had suddenly gone bananas, but we did the scene as he suggested with the result that the scene was twice as effective as it had been with all that dialogue. And Hitch was able to enjoy the symphony without interruption.' With only the one Hitchcock film on release in 1956 Stewart was reckoned to be the 'number three' box-office star behind John Wayne (second) and William Holden.

After such a sustained string of hits it came as something of a surprise that a seemingly ideal Stewart vehicle like *The Spirit of St. Louis* should have failed. Director Billy Wilder had considered casting John Kerr as the pioneer aviator and national hero Charles Lindbergh. Stewart eventually convinced all concerned of his eligibility despite being twenty years too old for the man being depicted. Wilder spent $6 million in recreating Lindbergs's 1927 non-stop flight from New York to Paris, fleshing out the journey with flashback vignettes capturing the flyer's boyish enthusiasm and comic escapades en route to his historic adventure. The film belongs

65

to Stewart's tour-de-force performance and the musical score by Franz Waxman. Stewart enlivens the potentially dull situation of a lengthy, one-man flight by investing his hero with doubt, despair, exhaustion and the jubilation as he senses the victory of his achievement. Wilder used locations along the original route including Nova Scotia, Ireland and a reconstruction of Le Bourget airfield in Paris. This painstaking search for authenticity met with public antipathy, and the studio head, Jack L.Warner, called it 'the most disastrous failure we ever had'. It was reported that the film did not take enough in a week in Lindbergh's birthplace to cover the staff's wages. Billy Wilder has said: 'We had unbelievable mechanical problems. Well, we could not communicate with a plane when it was up there. So when we had to do another take, it had to land, get the instructions, and take off again. We had other planes in the air to film the plane we were shooting. God, it was horrendous. The weather would change from one minute to the next. I never should have made this picture. It needed a director like John Frankenheimer, a man with an enormous patience for technical details.'

Stewart's other 1957 production, *Night Passage*, was a routine oater first seen as another collaboration with Anthony Mann but actually directed by James Neilson. Here James Stewart is a railroad cop, Grant McLaine, who is put in charge of the transport of the railroad payroll and thus allowed a second chance to prove his worth. Outlaw Whitey Harbin (Dan Duryea) and his gang also have designs on the money and plan a hijack. Among the gang members is the Utica Kid (Audie Murphy), McLaine's younger brother. In a final shoot-out the Utica Kid feels that blood takes paramountcy and sides with his brother, paying for his loyalty with his life. McLaine succeeds in reaching the railroad work-gang with their wages. Stewart's accordion playing gives a lift to a standard tale and caused the New York *Times* to comment, 'Actually, it is the presence of Mr Stewart in the show that gives it a personality above that of the average Western film. It is comforting to watch Mr Stewart upholding the truthful and good'. *The Spirit of St. Louis* and *Night Passage* were both box-office disappointments, and when the list of top box-office stars for 1957 was announced the emergence of a younger generation was strongly felt; the 'number one' attraction was Rock Hudson with Pat Boone and Elvis Presley also in the top five. Stewart managed a respectable eighth position just ahead of Jerry Lewis.

66

Vertigo now marked Stewart's final appearance for Alfred Hitchcock and it is one of the director's most celebrated films. 'Scottie' Ferguson (Stewart) is a San Francisco policeman who retires from the force suffering from acrophobia (fear of heights). An old college friend hires him to follow his wife Madeleine (Kim Novak) with whom Scottie falls instantly and helplessly in love. Madeleine is apparently possessed by the spirit of a long-dead ancestor and is drawn to the notion of suicide. Scottie takes her to the Mission at San Juan Batista hoping to unravel the mystery surrounding her. She rushes to the top of the Mission tower and plunges to her death. Scottie's fear of heights had prevented him from following her and, as a result, he suffers a breakdown. Several years later he meets Judy, Madeleine's double (Novak again), and begins to remodel her as an exact duplicate. However, Judy had been hired to impersonate the real Madeleine who was thrown from the tower by her husband. Scottie returns to the Mission Tower with Judy and forces himself to climb the steps as Judy breaks down and admits the truth and also that she loves Scottie. The sudden appearance of a nun startles Judy who plunges to her death and Scottie once again is left alone.

The audacious plotline of *Vertigo* is almost secondary to the themes and texture of the film. Stewart's fine portrayal of the detective is a testament to his emotional versatility as he paints an uncharacteristically dour and cruel picture of a man on an obsessive quest for the woman of his dreams. His actions are triggered by lust and a selfish compulsion to own the embodiment of his every desire. The blank-faced allure of Kim Novak is effectively utilised in a role once intended for Vera Miles whilst Bernard Herrman's music and Robert Burks' photography all make their contribution to a great tale of suspense and a classic study of male perversity. Stewart and 'Hitch' remained firm friends until the director's death in 1980 and discussed further projects but were never to work together again; *Vertigo* is an impeccable swansong.

Stewart was teamed with Kim Novak again in *Bell, Book and Candle*, an amiable screen version of John Van Druten's 1950 play. He is a New York book publisher, Shepherd Henderson, whose attraction to witch Gillian Holroyd (Novak) causes her to develop into a human being with the ability to blush, cry and love. Rex Harrison originated the Stewart role but refused the film version when Novak was announced as his possible co-star. A merry supporting cast includes Jack Lemmon, Ernie Kovacs, Hermione Gingold and Elsa Lanchester.

When the top money-making stars of 1958 were announced Stewart was the oldest member of the 'top ten' alongside youngsters like Brigitte Bardot and Jerry Lewis. He was fifty.

Chapter 7

Stewart had continued his involvement with the military as an active member of the Air Force Reserve and was promoted to the rank of Brigadier-General in July 1959 despite a widely publicised campaign of opposition by Senator Margaret Chase, who seemed to think he had been promoted because he was a celebrity rather than on merit. On screen he topped off his most productive decade with two big successes; *Anatomy of A Murder* and *The FBI Story*.

In *Anatomy of a Murder* Stewart plays defense lawyer Paul Biegler, a choice role in an Otto Preminger production which marked an advance for adult stories and frankness in the American cinema. In a small Michigan city Frederick Manion (Ben Gazzara) is charged with the murder of a bartender. Manion defends his actions, claiming that he was enraged by the bartender's attack and rape of his wife Laura (Lee Remick). The case comes to trial and turns into a showdown between the defense and the prosecution attorney, Claude Dancer (George C. Scott). Dancer asserts that Laura had willingly flirted with the bartender and subsequently been beaten by her husband who went on to murder her lover. Biegler wins sympathy for the couple and manages to win the case for Manion who is judged to have acted on an 'irresistible impulse'. Despite his achievement Biegler is unable to collect his fee as the couple have quickly left town.

A quarter of a century on *Anatomy of a Murder* can be seen to be a film with flaws; its running time of two hours and forty minutes is excessive and the alleged daring of its subject-matter has inevitably dated. Nevertheless it remains a powerful show window for the acting talents of a strong cast, none more so than Stewart as a wily, cunning and cagey lawyer whose modest demeanour belies his court-room expertise. "I'm just a simple country lawyer," he tells the jury. Many of Stewart's long-standing fans complained at the presence of their favourite star in a film dealing openly with rape, but Stewart believed that it was too good a role to pass over although he did recall the reaction of his father: 'A travelling salesman happened to remark to my Dad, "Your son, Jim, just made a dirty picture". Well, Dad phoned me at four o'clock in the morning and I spent a half hour explaining what the film was about.

'When the film came to Indiana, he took an ad out in the local paper saying: "My son, Jim, has just made a nasty picture and I advise no-one to go and see it." Well, of course, the film did much more business than it would have done otherwise. Later on I found that Dad had sneaked into a drive-in screening of the film to see it for himself. The next day he phoned me again at four o'clock in the morning to say that he didn't think it was dirty at all, that it was just fine."

The film's 'daring' reputation gave a boost to its already potent ticket sales and the film grossed in excess of $5 million in America. Stewart was named Best Actor by the New York Film Critics and at the Venice Film Festival, whilst receiving also his fifth Academy Award nomination. At the Oscars he faced competition from Laurence Harvey (*Room at the Top*), Jack Lemmon (*Some Like it Hot*), Paul Muni (*The Last Angry Man*) and the winner Charlton Heston (*Ben-Hur*). *Anatomy of a Murder* was nominated in seven categories, including Best Picture but was mentioned in none of the winners' envelopes; *Ben-Hur* swept the board with an unprecedented eleven awards.

The *FBI Story*, like *Strategic Air Command*, presents a glorification of the work of a powerful American institution as seen through the eyes of one ordinary citizen. Stewart is an agent, Chip Hardesty, whose twenty-five year career of law enforcement fortuitously coin-cides with the rise of the Federal Bureau of Investigation. Thus we witness him lecturing the new recruits on his involvement in the apprehension of Baby Face Nelson, his fight with the Ku Klux Klan in the South, with the post-war Communist threat, et al. Vera Miles is his faithful if occasionally doubting wife who realises that his first love will always be the Bureau.

A film which could only be preaching to the converted, *The FBI Story* was hindered by its length (149 minutes) and its inherently episodic format. However, *Variety* felt that it was aided by Stewart's 'restrained performance, wry and intelligent, completely credible as the film covers a span of about 25 years to show both the fledgling agent and the older man'.

On the strength of *Anatomy of a Murder* and *FBI Story* Stewart was judged the 'number three' box-office star behind Rock Hudson and Cary Grant.

Stewart next chose to lend his name to a modest and somewhat dour anti-war statement *The Mountain Road* in which his character, Major Baldwin, learns the responsibility of power and compassion in the war-torn China of 1944. The film, Stewart's only release in 1960, was poorly received.

In 1961 he provided the narration for *X-15*, a drama about researchers at Edwards Air Force Missile Base in California; and he was seen on screen in *Two Rode Together*, his first film for the director John Ford. In this Stewart is the cynical Tascosa marshall Guthrie McCabe whose one abiding principle is—what's in it for me? Lieutenant Jim Gary (Richard Widmark) demands his co-operation in an attempt by the cavalry to retrieve hostages held by the Comanches for many years. McCabe refuses until he is offered $500 per captive. Trading rifles, McCabe frees the white boy, Running Wolf, and the Mexican girl Elena (Linda Cristal) but not before he is forced to kill warrior Stone Calf (Woody Strode). Back at the fort the return of the captives is not the joyous event that had been anticipated. Elena is publicly shunned and Running Wolf, having killed the woman who claims him as her son, is lynched by the mob. McCabe is disgusted by the treatment of Elena and, when his job is usurped by his deputy, he leaves with her in search of better days.

Two Rode Together is a mildly engaging, lazily conceived entertainment with Stewart's geniality making McCabe's frank corruptibility the more acceptable. He appears however to have warmed to Ford's abrasive directorial style. 'The set was anything by tranquil on a Ford picture,' he has said. 'Ford believed that acting is a competitive thing. That it's good to be tense, good to be suspicious of other actors. His direction would be mostly, whispers. I remember on the first picture I did with him, he sidled up to me on the first day or so — Richard Widmark was in the picture and we'd never worked together before — and said, "Now this Widmark is a pretty good actor. I've seen him do some awfully good things. And he's got a pretty good part in this and if I were you I'd watch him. He'll start grabbing stuff away from you so keep your eye on him and keep on your toes."

'So, I said, "alright". And nothing more was aid. But after the picture was over Dick Widmark and I were talking and it turned out that he'd gone to Widmark and said exactly the same thing about me! This way of keeping everything on a critical basis was his way of working and it was very effective.'

Stewart worked with Ford again the following year to better advantage in *The Man Who Shot Liberty Valance*. He plays a man who rises to be a Senator on the skill of another man's sharp-shooting. Made in black and white the film uses Stewart and John Wayne as archetypes of what they represented on screen; Stewart youthful, idealistic with a stubborn streak; Wayne, dignified, capable and on the side of right. The story is told in flashback as Senator Ranse Stoddard (Stewart) and his wife Hallie (Vera Miles) return to the town of Shinbone for the funeral of Tom Doniphan (Wayne). The year is 1910 but many years earlier Stoddard was a tenderfoot lawyer intent on bringing justice into the area. He was beaten and bullied into a showdown with notorious gunslinger Liberty Valance (Lee Marvin). Hallie had begged Tom to intervene fully aware that Ranse faced certain death. At the gunfight several shots are exchanged and Valance is killed with Ranse hailed as a hero and nominated for Congress as 'the man who shot Liberty Valance'. Ranse hesitated, feeling that to build a career on a killing would negate all his principles. It was then that Tom came forward to admit that he shot Valance from the sidelines out of love for Hallie. Ranse went on to a career in the Senate and marriage to Hallie, whilst Tom grew old alone and died.

The film writer Allen Eyles has hailed *The Man Who Shot Liberty Valance* in saying: 'No film has more eloquently depicted the taming of the West, the repression of individual liberty for the sake of the community and the nation, and the cost in human terms'. It is Ford's last great Western and was modestly popular on its release, grossing $4 million domestically; but Stewart's other 1962 films gave less cause for celebration; he is one of the many stars in the sprawling Cinerama epic *How the West Was Won* as fur trapper Linus Rawlings;

72

In John Ford's The Man Who Shot Liberty Valance, *with Vera Miles, John Wayne and Woody Strode.*

Crisis in Take Her, She's Mine *(1963).*

Young Philip Alford gets a 16th-birthday cake in Andrew V. McLaglen's Shenandoah.

73

while *Mr Hobbs Takes A Vacation* finds him as a harassed father and husband whose hopes for a peaceful vacation are quickly shattered by the comic complications he is led into by his family. *Variety* felt that 'the picture has its stauchest ally in Stewart, whose acting instincts are so remarkably keen that he can instill amusement into scenes that otherwise threaten to fall flat'. His work was acknowledged with a Silver Bear Award as Best Actor at the 1962 Berlin Film Festival.

Age tends to restrict an actor's options. Stewart was now 54, and so becoming less acceptable for parts as a romantic leading man. As a result, his work in the early 1960s seemed increasingly reliant on formulistic film-making whether in the field of domestic comedy or the Western genre. The family feeling emanating from the Hollywood of his youth and the sense of security engendered by the studio system were gone. Close friends like Clark Gable, Humphrey Bogart and Gary Cooper were dead. Being a freelance performer in an industry of shrinking opportunities was not easy and who could blame him for choosing the safe options? *Take Her, She's Mine* is unworthy of him, a negligible comedy in which he mugs his way through a strained farce as a lawyer concerned about his college-age daughter and her involvement with the 'wrong crowd', i.e. Ban the Bomb demonstrators and beatniks. Stewart's participation in John Ford's *Cheyenne Autumn* was limited to a cameo role in a broadly comic sequence as a corrupt Wyatt Earp. It allowed the actor further first-hand experience of the director's 'planned improvisation'. 'In a Ford film you were never exactly sure of what was going to happen. His crew knew exactly what was going to happen. His assistants knew exactly what was going to happen. The only people who didn't know were the actors', Stewart has revealed. 'In *Cheyenne Autumn* Arthur Kennedy and I had to go bursting out of a bar and get in a stationary wagon with a team of horses. 200 people were outside in the street. Ford said to me, "Now I want you to both rush out and get into the wagon, take the reins and go out to the left".

'Well, he'd had his assistant tell all the people in the crowd that I was going to turn and go in the opposite direction. So when I changed into these people they were completely surprised. They shrieked and ran and men grabbed women to get them out of the way. People were yelling and shouting 'Go the other way' and, of course, it was complete bedlam. But it looked just great on the screen. It was exactly what he wanted.'

74

Dear Brigitte was another example of genially cosy domestic fare with Stewart as Professor Robert Leaf, understandably perturbed by the advanced development of his eight-year-old son Erasmus (Billy Mumy), a mathematical genius with a passion for Brigitte Bardot; but it was totally eclipsed by his other 1965 films, especially *Shenandoah*, which was the first film he made with Andrew V.McLaglen as director. A Civil War saga, *Shenandoah* captures the fratricidal conflict in human terms as it depicts the effects on one family. Stewart is isolationist Virginia farmer Charlie Anderson who has never owned a slave and is solely concerned with the well-being of his clan and their hard-earned prosperity. Yet the consequences of the war are unavoidable; the youngest of his six sons is captured by Yankee troops who believe him to be a Confederate. Charlie and four of his sons go in search of the boy, encountering the war at first hand. Back at the ranch the remaining son and his wife are killed by Confederate looters. Charlie's search is futile, made up of moments of fear, unexpected danger and frustration. Returning home the remainder of the family go to church for Sunday services and during the hymns the missing boy stumbles in on crutches and the fragments of the family are reunited.

Stewart's family-head in *Shenandoah* is his best film work of the 1960s. In a poignant drama that effectively personalises an epic rupture of a nation he exudes his best qualities of paternal sincerity, giving added conviction and nobility to a man who doesn't want to be involved but suffers nonetheless. *Newsweek* reviewed the film in August 1965: 'What Stewart himself achieves must be a source of some discouragement as well as instruction for the young, unskilled actors working with him. He is far from young. His role of paterfamilias is more tired than his eyes. Yet Stewart compels belief with his strength and simplicity.'

In *The Flight of the Phoenix*, released in 1965, Stewart was given an off-beat piece of casting as old-style pilot Frank Towns in an all-star desert survival drama. When his plane crashes in the Sahara, Towns takes full responsibility despite the negligence of his drunken navigator Lew Moran (Richard Attenborough). The passengers are a group of oil-company workers en route to a new posting and as the burning heat and isolation take their toll nerves are frayed and tempers flare. After many days the men realise that their only chance of survival is to follow the engineering plans of a German designer

Heinrich Dorfmann (Hardy Kruger) who hopes to use the remainder of their crashed plane to build a new craft. Towns opposes the plan but acknowledges his mistake and flies everyone to safety.

The Flight of the Phoenix is sustained throughout its 157 minutes by the choice acting of a cast that includes Peter Finch, Ernest Borgnine, Dan Duryea and Ian Bannen. Stewart gives a commendable display of character acting and analysed his role thus: 'My character's sort of a sad man in a way. I felt he was a man who had been passed by, by the modern jet airplanes and the computerised systems and automation. He doesn't want it that way. He wants to run the machine, he doesn't want the machine to run him'.

Shenandoah was one of 1965's most popular films, grossing over $7 million domestically, and, combines with *The Flight of the Phoenix* and *Dear Brigitte* restored Stewart to his former standing amongst the top-ten box-office starts. He was eighth, and ahead of Elizabeth Taylor and Richard Burton.

Chapter 8

Stewart obviously felt so much at home riding the range that he spent most of his remaining years as a leading man in the saddle. Immediately following *Shenandoah* there was talk of an 'untitled story about an ex-major league baseball pitcher's adventures in Japan and his regeneration', there were also plans for a Warner Brothers film; 'Eighth Air Force', which similarly came to nought. A few years later he observed; "You just can't find a good comedy script anymore, I don't think they're written'. The film he did make was *The Rare Breed*, a second work with Andrew V. McLaglen. 'I had seen some of his television work and heard about him from John Ford, with whom he has served his apprenticeship,' Stewart explained. 'He tells stories about being on the set even as a tiny child when his father, Victor McLaglen, was making *The Informer* for Ford. Anyway, Andy became assistant to Ford and I reckon there is no better training ground. He works a lot like Ford, uses the camera the same way, has the same feeling for getting excitement and vitality on to the screen. That's why I like him.'

The Rare Breed has Maureen O'Hara as an indomitable widow, Martha Evans, who sells her prize white-faced Hereford bull at the 1884 St Louis Stockman's Exposition. Stewart is a cowhand, Sam Burnett, who delivers the animal to its new owner Alexander Brown (Brian Keith) in Dodge City. Martha and her daughter Hilary (Juliet Mills) travel with Sam to see out their belief that the Hereford can be crossbred with the native longhorn stock. At the ranch a romantic rivalry develops between Sam and Brown over Martha; Brown scoffs at her cross-breeding notions but Sam has faith. Come the Spring Martha's bull is dead but Sam discovers a longhorn cow with a Hereford calf, and together they rejoice over the first of the 'rare breed'. While the plotline of *The Rare Breed* is of interest, the other aspects of the film are undistinguished.

Firecreek, in 1967, was a marginal improvement; it is a dour tale of a small-town sheriff Johnny Cobb (Stewart) whose peaceable outlook on life is sorely challenged with the arrival in town of a desperado Larkin (Henry Fonda) and his gang of outlaws. Cobb is slow to anger and takes a tolerant view of the gang's activities, unsuccessfully attempting to combat their presence with logic and quiet reason. Tension grows and Cobb is forced into a showdown, emerging wounded but victorious with help from Evelyn Pittman (Inger Stevens) who kills Larkin when Cobb is too incapacitated to continue the struggle.

Stewart's one Western for 1968 was *Bandolero!*, a jovial piece of nonsense with Stewart and Dean Martin as outlaw brothers ruthlessly pursued by Sheriff Johnson (George Kennedy) and his posse. Dee Bishop (Martin) is wanted for the murder of a rancher in a bank hold-up and also for the kidnapping of the rancher's widow Maria (Raquel Welch). The Sheriff's awkward love for Maria keeps him intent on tracking down the brothers. In Mexico the Bishops are captured but released to help Johnson withstand an attack by Mexican bandits in which both Dee and the bank-robber Mace (Stewart) are killed. The film was shot on location in Texas throughout the autumn of 1967 and received a world premiere in Dallas on 18 June, 1968. Stewart attended the function, telling reporters; "It's part of your job. It gets a picture started and I enjoy getting out to different parts of the country and meeting people who show a genuine interest in pictures and picture people".

Stewart did not make a film in 1968; in February of that year he was honoured for his contribution to the cinema alongside Mervyn LeRoy and Mae West at the 30th Annual Awards of the Delta Kappa Alpha cinema fraternity chapter at the University of Southern California. He went to Vietnam to meet the men and sign authographs, and toured military bases during his final two weeks of duty before being retired, aged 60, as a Brigadier-General in the Air Force Reserve. He received the Distinguished Service Medal and a citation which read, 'the singularly distinctive accomplishments of General

78

Stewart culminate a long and distinguished career in the service of his country and reflect the highest credit upon himself and the US Air Force'.

The Stewart family suffered a personal tragedy in June 1969 when Gloria's son Ronald was killed in action in Vietnam, at the age of twenty-four. In 1970 Stewart commented: "Neither my wife nor I have any bitterness. We've gotten hundreds and hundreds of letters. I believe in the cause he died for. The war has been a trial, and a tremendously difficult thing for the nation. But if there is a tragedy about it, it is the national tragedy that there has been so much sacrifice without a unified nation behind the cause'.

When the Stewarts received the news of Ronald's death the actor was in the midst of filming *The Cheyenne Social Club*, a comedy Western with Henry Fonda as co-star and Gene Kelly as director. The basic premise of the plot involves the actors as two wandering cowpokes who come into a special inheritance — a brothel. As the odd couple of the old West the duo display some engaging teamwork in a mildly ribald self-mocking romp. Stewart's trusty steed Pie made his last appearance in the film. The actor had refused to ride any other horse throughout his Western career and felt that the animal had a second sense about film-making. Unknown to Stewart Henry Fonda captured the horse in watercolour during the filming of *The Cheyenne Social Club* and the portrait hangs in the actor's library.

The 1970s found Stewart active in many fields outside the cinema, so that *Fools' Parade* in 1971 was his last film for five years. He worked for a reported fee of $250,000 and 10% of gross takings in a project which he himself put into production. 'It was such a pure, honest kind of story,' he explained. 'The good guys against the bad guys; pure melodrama.' The good guys are led by Stewart as Mattie Appleyard, one of three convicts released from a West Virginia jail in 1935. He plans to open a store and go straight having saved his prison earnings of forty years, a grand total of $25,452. There are, of course, complications — the cheque can only be cashed in a town that Mattie is legally prevented from entering and the sadistic prison warder, Doc Council (George Kennedy), is intent on seeing that he does not obtain the money. Mattie rigs himself us as a walking bomb and threatens to blow up the bank and then kills Doc in the ensuing pursuit. Arrested and put on trial he is cleared and freely allowed to enter the bank.

'Stewart spent most of his remaining years as a leading man in the saddle' _ The Rare Breed *(1966) and* Firecreek *(1967)*.

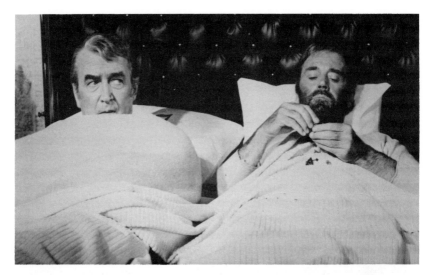

Stewart unwillingly shares a bed with Henry Fonda in The Cheyenne Social Club
(1970).

James Stewart in his TV series Hawkins, *a role reminscent of his Paul Biegler in*
Anatomy of a Murder.

Mattie Appleyard is a quintessential Stewart hero: a man of principle stubbornly determined to stand his ground, and modest with it. 'I'm just an American coming into a bank to cash a cheque,' he asserts. The film itself is delightfully idiosyncratic and satisfying — Stewart has a glass eye which he takes evident enjoyment in removing at key moments — and there is a quirky feeling to the whole yarn.

In 1970 Stewart had returned to the Broadway stage as Elwood P.Dowd in *Harvey*, feeling that twenty extra years had ripened him for the role. The critics and audiences agreed whilst Stewart commented, 'I welcomed the change. My wife, Gloria, and I found ourselves sitting around Beverly Hills having conversations with our dogs. Hollywood is a little quiet and depressing right now, it's another of our disaster times'. Then, at the start of the 1971/2 television season, his first weekly series appeared, 'The Jimmy Stewart Show'.

Stewart had been no stranger to the small screen. In the 1950s he appeared in several half-hour dramas and also served as director on *The Trail to Christmas* in 1957, the Western adaption of Charles Dickens' *A Christmas Carol*. In 1962 John Ford directed him in *Flashing Spikes* as ballplayer Slim Conway; and he has been a frequent star on 'The Dean Martin Show' and 'The Jack Benny Show'. 'The Jimmy Stewart Show', however, despite a reputed million dollar fee, was an ill-advised move. The half-hour series was a throwback to his domestic comedies of the early 1960s with Stewart as absent-minded professor Jim Howard, head of a large and trouble-ridden family. The series lasted one season and twenty-four episodes.

In 1972 *Harvey* was adapted into a television special and filmed with Helen Hayes as Dowd's sister Veta and, in 1973, Stewart made a second, superior attempt at a television series; *Hawkins on Murder*. Stewart's country-boy lawyer Billy Jim Hawkins is a variant on his Paul Biegler from *Anatomy of a Murder* and the subsequent one-season series plunged him into a number of cases with 'adult' themes, adult at least for American television. The segment 'Murder in Movieland', for example, finds Hawkins examining murder among the homosexual community of Hollywood, and it caused the New York *Times* to salute Hawkins as 'the most impressively acted, written, directed and photographed of the new series so far this season'. Stewart won the Golden Globe Award as Best Television actor for his role.

The Shootist – *James Stewart as Dr Hosteler tells gunfighter J.B. Books (John Wayne) that he is dying of cancer.*

Any actor can point to a string of roles he might have played or films that he missed out on. Stewart is no exception; he had actively sought the lead in Hitchcock's *North By Northwest*, could have been in *The Longest Day* or co-starred with Marilyn Monroe in *Let's Make Love*, and was announced for *The Way West* with Kirk Douglas and Burt Lancaster. The casualty which gives him the greatest cause for regret is *The Streets of Laredo* which would have teamed him with Henry Fonda and John Wayne. The film was the brainchild of director Peter Bogdanovich who prepared a script with Larry McMurty, his partner on *The Last Picture Show* in 1971. The script was never filmed despite two attempts to put it on screen. Stewart explained; 'I read it and wasn't impressed. I called Duke and asked him what he thought. He said, "Jimmy boy, they're trying to make three old fogies out of us". And he was right. So we all turned it down.' Another role he rejected was the old Claude Rains part in the new version of *Mr Smith* now adapted into *Billy Jack Goes to Washington* (1977).

Stewart did achieve one long-standing ambition, however, when he brought *Harvey* to London's West End in 1975. 'You know it sounds a bit of a cliché', he said at the time, 'but to act on the London stage has been my greatest ambition ever since I was a young actor in New York forty years ago.' Asked why he appeared to have retired from the screen he replied, 'I just don't seem to fit in any more. Some of the scripts I am sent bewilder me'.

He did return for a string of unchallenging cameo roles; as John Wayne's doctor in the elegiac, poignant *The Shootist* (1976); as the wealthy owner of the hardware in peril in *Airport '77* with Jack Lemmon; as the frail Colonel Sternwood in the botched remake of *The Big Sleep* (1978); and as the grandfather in *The Magic of Lassie* (1978). The latter film even finds the actor croaking a few tunes and displaying undiminished professionalism as he brings aching sincerity to a small-scale, folksy saga of sentimentality.

The Green Horizon (1981), filmed in Kenya, was little seen but generally considered a disaster, and summarised by Leonard Maltin's *TV Movies* thus: 'Pilot (Philip Sayer) crashes plane into wilds of Africa, comes upon game preserve occupied by Stewart and granddaughter. Even old Jimmy is boring'. A cable project, *Right of Way*, with Bette Davis, marked a partial return to form. They offer touching portrayals of septuagenarians Mini and Teddy Dwyer who

Stewart as the millionaire philanthropist in Airport '77.

plan a joint-suicide when Mini is diagnosed as having a terminal blood disease. Their daughter and the authorities intervene to block their scheme but they are not to be swayed, achieving a dignified exit, together. In interviews Stewart said; "Bette is a fascinating, warm, considerate person, and during filming of *Right of Way* she was absolutely exhilarating from the first to the last day. Both Bette and I though it was worth doing. It's a good, well-written story about something I think is very important." In its completed form *Right of Way* is a somewhat mawkish and maudlin film which handles its subject-matter awkwardly and with uneasy humour, but sincerity too. Stewart certainly comes off best in his most interesting role for a long while, which *Variety* noted as the 'sensitivity and conviction' which he brought to the part, qualities in a Stewart performance that have remained unchanged over half a century.

Perhaps the key to Stewart's durability is that he has always played himself. However, within that framework he has essayed a remarkable range of individuals, suggesting, through the subtle nuances of his style, characters as diverse as the fumbling cowpoke in *Destry Rides Again* and the immoral opportunist of John Ford's *Two Rode Together*. It was Ford who pinpointed Stewart's appeal when he observed, 'Audiences just like him'.

Stewart's health in recent years has been poor; he now wears a hearing aid, has a heart condition and sciatica and was treated for skin cancer in 1983. In 1982 it was announced that he would play the title role of a small-town doctor and mayor in a further television series 'His Honor, Doc Potter'. It was reported that Stewart's fee would be $350,000 for a two-hour pilot programme and $40,000 per episode if a series resulted. Whatever the reasons 'His Honor, Doc Potter' was never made and Stewart has no intention of returning to the rigours of weekly television.

In 1984 he began work on a cable television project, *The Late Christopher Bean*, for director George Schaefer. Sidney Howard's stage hit, based on René Fauchois' *Prenez Garde à la Peinture*, had previously been filmed in 1933 with Lionel Barrymore and Marie Dressler in the roles now intended for Stewart and co-star Carol Burnett. Described as a 'comedy of an avaricious family whose housekeeper is the custodian of a posthumously famous artist's paintings', *The Late Christopher Bean* was cancelled when Carol Burnett fell ill on the sixth day of rehearsals prior to filming.

However, Stewart continues to plan for the future; 'I still read scripts, maybe one, two, three a month. But you jus' have to realise this age thing is very important, and there aren't as many grandfather parts as other parts. And now I've put my foot down. The minute I see a script and I get to the bit where my character is introduced and they say "He's a rather grouchy old man", then I slam the script shut and send it back. Why do they say, because you're old you have to be grouchy? I don't know. Waal, it puzzles me, let's say. I refuse to play a grouchy old man!'

He may make another dozen films or he may never film again – it is immaterial; his place in the highest ranks of Hollywood screen actors is unassailable, his work is durable, constantly on view, and tributes still pour in. In 1980 he was honoured with the American Film Institute Life Achievement Award in a ceremony hosted by Henry Fonda at the Beverly Hilton Hotel. Grace Kelly flew in from Monaco and the actor received warm tributes from many colleagues and friends. 'It's kind of like tying a happy ribbon around a wonderful lifetime that has blessed me by letting me get paid doing work I love to do,' he declared.

In 1982 he was feted at the Berlin Film Festival for his contribution to the cinema and his seventy-fifth birthday was celebrated in his hometown with three days of events including a film festival, a five-foot birthday cake and the erection of a nine-foot statue. The recent revivals of his four productions with Alfred Hitchcock – *Rope*, *Rear Window*, *The Man Who Knew Too Much* and *Vertigo* – have produced a fresh wave of acclaim world-wide, and in 1985 freshly-minted prints of *The Glenn Miller Story*, with a stereo soundtrack, will be used to give the film a major re-release in cinemas, a venture which Stewart intends to help promote by travelling around. At the age of seventy-six he does not even contemplate retirement: 'My job has been my life. It has made a wonderful life for me. To say I am going to retire and walk away from it wouldn't seem fair'.

The Films of James Stewart

THE MURDER MAN (1935). Dir: *Tim Whelan.* Cast: *Spencer Tracy, Virginia Bruce, Lionel Atwill, Harvey Stephens, Robert Barrat.* 70 mins.

ROSE MARIE (1936). Dir: *W.S. Van Dyke II.* Cast: *Jeanette MacDonald, Nelson Eddy, Reginald Owen, Allan Jones, Una O'Connor, David Niven.* 113 mins.

NEXT TIME WE LOVE (1936). Dir: *Edward H. Griffiths.* Cast: *Margaret Sullavan, Ray Milland, Grant Mitchell, Anna Demetrio, Robert McWade.* 87 mins.

WIFE VERSUS SECRETARY (1936). Dir: *Clarence Brown.* Cast: *Clark Gable, Jean Harlow, Myrna Loy, May Robson, Hobart Cavanaugh, George Barbier.* 88 mins.

SMALL TOWN GIRL (1936). Dir: *William A. Wellman.* Cast: *Janet Gaynor, Robert Taylor, Binnie Barnes, Lewis Stone, Elizabeth Patterson.* 90 mins.

SPEED (1936). Dir: *Edwin L.Marin.* Cast: *Wendy Barrie, Una Merkel, Weldon Heyburn, Ted Healy, Patricia Wilder, Ralph Morgan, Robert Livingston.* 72 mins.

THE GEORGEOUS HUSSY (1936). Dir: *Clarence Brown.* Cast: *Joan Crawford, Robert Taylor, Lionel Barrymore, Franchot Tone, Melvyn Douglas.* 102 mins.

BORN TO DANCE (1936). Dir: *Roy Del Ruth.* Cast: *Eleanor Powell, Virginia Bruce, Una Merkel, Sid Silvers, Frances Langford, Raymond Walburn.* 108 mins.

AFTER THE THIN MAN (1936). Dir: *W.S. Van Dyke II.* Cast: *William Powell, Myrna Loy, Elissa Landi, Joseph Calleia, Jessie Ralph, Alan Marshall.* 112 mins.

SEVENTH HEAVEN (1937). Dir: *Henry King*. Cast: *Simone Simon, Jean Hersholt, Gregory Ratoff, Gale Sondergaard, J. Edward Bromberg, John Qualen*. 102 mins.

THE LAST GANGSTER (1937). Dir: *Edward Ludwig*. Cast: *Edward G. Robinson, Rose Stradner, Lionel Stander, Douglas Scott, John Carradine, Sidney Blackmer*. 81 mins.

NAVY BLUE AND GOLD (1937). Dir: *Sam Wood*. Cast: *Robert Young, Lionel Barrymore, Florence Rice, Billie Burke, Tom Brown, Samuel S. Hinds, Paul Kelly*. 94 mins.

OF HUMAN HEARTS (1938). Dir: *Clarence Brown*. Cast: *Walter Huston, Beulah Bondi, Guy Kibbee, Charles D. Coburn, John Carradine, Ann Rutherford*. 105 mins.

VIVACIOUS LADY (1938). Dir: *George Stevens*. Cast: *Ginger Rogers, James Ellison, Charles Coburn, Beulah Bondi, Frances Mercer, Phyllis Kennedy*. 90 mins.

THE SHOPWORN ANGEL (1938). Dir: *H.C. Potter*. Cast: *Margaret Sullavan, Walter Pidgeon, Hattie McDaniel, Nat Pendleton, Alan Curtis, Sam Levene*. 85 mins.

YOU CAN'T TAKE IT WITH YOU (1938). Dir: *Frank Capra*. Cast: *Jean Arthur, Lionel Barrymore, Edward Arnold, Mischa Auer, Ann Miller*. 127 mins.

MADE FOR EACH OTHER (1939). Dir: *John Cromwell*. Cast: *Carole Lombard, Charles Coburn, Lucile Watson, Harry Davenport, Ruth Weston*. 90 mins.

THE ICE FOLLIES OF 1939 (1939). Dir: *Reinhold Schunzel*. Cast: *Joan Crawford, Lew Ayres, Lewis Stone, Bess Ehrhardt, Lionel Stander, Charles D. Brown*. 82 mins.

IT'S A WONDERFUL WORLD (1939). Dir: *W.S. Van Dyke II*. Cast: *Claudette Colbert, Guy Kibbee, Nat Pendleton, Frances Drake, Edgar Kennedy, Ernest Truex*. 86 mins.

MR SMITH GOES TO WASHINGTON (1939). Dir: *Frank Capra*. Cast: *Jean Arthur, Claude Rains, Edward Arnold, Guy Kibbee, Thomas Mitchell, Eugene Pallette*. 126 mins.

DESTRY RIDES AGAIN (1939). Dir: *George Marshall*. Cast: *Marlene Dietrich, Brian Donlevy, Mischa Auer, Charles Winninger, Allen Jenkins, Una Merkel*. 94 mins.

THE SHOP AROUND THE CORNER (1940). Dir: *Ernst Lubitsch*. Cast: *Margaret Sullavan, Frank Morgan, Joseph Schildkraut, Sara Haden, Felix Bressart*. 97 mins.

THE MORTAL STORM (1940). Dir: *Frank Borzage*. Cast: *Margaret Sullavan, Frank Morgan, Robert Young, Robert Stack, Bonita Granville, Dan Dailey Jr*. 100 mins.

NO TIME FOR COMEDY (1940). Dir: *William Keighley*. Cast: *Rosalind Russell, Genevieve Tobin, Charlie Ruggles, Allyn Joslin, Clarence Kolb*. 93 mins.

THE PHILADELPHIA STORY (1940). Dir: *George Cukor*. Cast: *Cary Grant, Katharine Hepburn, Ruth Hussey, John Howard, Roland Young, John Halliday*. 112 mins.

COME LIVE WITH ME (1941). Dir: *Clarence Brown*. Cast: *Hedy Lamarr, Ian Hunter, Verree Teasdale, Donald Meek, Barton MacLane, Edward Ashley*. 86 mins.

POT O'GOLD (1941). Dir: *George Marshall*. Cast: *Paulette Goddard, Horace Heidt and his Musical Knights, Charles Winninger, Mary Gordon, Frank Melton*. 86 mins.

ZIEGFELD GIRL *(1941)*. *Dir: Robert Z. Leonard*. Cast: *Judy Garland, Hedy Lamarr, Lana Turner, Tony Martin, Jackie Cooper, Ian Hunter, Charles Winninger*. 131 mins.

IT'S A WONDERFUL LIFE (1946). Dir: *Frank Capra*. Cast: *Donna Reed, Lionel Barrymore, Thomas Mitchell, Henry Travers, Beulah Bondi, Ward Bond*. 129 mins.

MAGIC TOWN (1947). Dir: *William A. Wellman*. Cast: *Jane Wyman, Kent Smith, Ned Sparks, Wallace Ford, Regis Toomey, Ann Doran, Donald Meek*. 103 mins.

CALL NORTHSIDE 777 (1948). Dir: *Henry Hathaway*. Cast: *Richard Conte, Lee J.Cobb, Helen Walker, Betty Garde, Kasia Orzazewski, Joanne de Bergh*. 111 mins

ON OUR MERRY WAY (1948). Dir: *John Huston/George Stevens*. Cast: *Burgess Meredith, Henry Fonda, Eduardo Ciannelli, Dorothy Ford, Carl Switzer*. 107 mins.

ROPE (1948). Dir: *Alfred Hitchcock*. Cast: *Farley Granger, John Dall, Joan Chandler, Sir Cedric Hardwicke, Constance Collier, Edith Evanson*. 81 mins.

YOU GOTTA STAY HAPPY (1948). Dir: *H.C. Potter*. Cast: *Joan Fontaine, Eddie Albert, Roland Young, Willard Parker, Percy Kilbride, Porter Hall*. 100 mins.

THE STRATTON STORY (1949). Dir: *Sam Wood*. Cast: *June Allyson, Frank Morgan, Agnes Moorehead, Bill Williams, Bruce Cowling, Cliff Clark*. 106 mins.

MALAYA (1949). Dir: *Richard Thorpe*. Cast: *Spencer Tracy, Valentina Cortese, Sidney Greenstreet, John Hodiak, Lionel Barrymore, Gilbert Roland*. 98 mins.

WINCHESTER '73 (1950). Dir: *Anthony Mann*. Cast: *Shelley Winters, Dan Duryea, Stephen McNally, Millard Mitchell, Charles Drake, John McIntire*. 92 mins.

BROKEN ARROW (1950). Dir: *Delmer Daves*. Cast: *Jeff Chandler, Debra Paget, Basil Ruysdael, Will Geer, Joyce MacKenzie, Arthur Hunnicutt*. 93 mins.

THE JACKPOT (1950). Dir: *Walter Lang*. Cast: *Barbara Hale, James Gleason, Fred Clark, Alan Mowbray, Patricia Medina, Natalie Wood, Tommy Rettig*. 87 mins.

HARVEY (1950). Dir: *Henry Koster*. Cast: *Josephine Hull, Peggy Dow, Charles Drake, Cecil Kellaway, Victoria Horne, Jesse White, William Lynn*. 104 mins.

NO HIGHWAY (1951). Dir: *Henry Koster*. Cast: *Marlene Dietrich, Glynis Johns, Jack Hawkins, Janette Scott, Ronald Squire, Elizabeth Allan*. 99 mins.

THE GREATEST SHOW ON EARTH (1952). Dir: *Cecil B. De Mille*. Cast: *Betty Hutton, Cornel Wilde, Charlton Heston, Dorothy Lamour, Gloria Grahame*. 153 mins.

BEND OF THE RIVER (1952). Dir: *Anthony Mann*. Cast: *Arthur Kennedy, Julia Adams, Rock Hudson, Lori Nelson, Jay C. Flippen, Chubby Johnson*. 91 mins.

CARBINE WILLIAMS (1952). Dir: *Richard Thorpe*. Cast: *Jean Hagen, Wendell Corey, Carl Benton Reid, Paul Stewart, Otto Hullet, Rhys Williams*. 91 mins.

THE NAKED SPUR (1953). Dir: *Anthony Mann*. Cast: *Robert Ryan, Janet Leigh, Ralph Meeker, Millard Mitchell*. 91 mins.

THUNDER BAY (1953). Dir: *Anthony Mann*. Cast: *Joanne Dru, Gilbert Roland, Dan Duryea, Marcia Henderson, Jay C. Flippen, Antonio Moreno*. 102 mins.

THE GLENN MILLER STORY (1953). Dir: *Anthony Mann*. Cast: *June Allyson, Henry Morgan, Charles Drake, George Tobias, Barton MacLane, Sig Ruman*. 116 mins.

REAR WINDOW (1954). Dir: *Alfred Hitchcock*. Cast: *Grace Kelly, Wendell Corey, Thelma Ritter, Raymond Burr, Judith Evelyn, Ross Bagdasarian*. 122 mins.

THE FAR COUNTRY (1955). Dir: *Anthony Mann*. Cast: *Ruth Roman, Corinne Calvert, Walter Brennan, John McIntire, Jay C. Flippen, Henry Morgan*. 97 mins.

STRATEGIC AIR COMMAND (1955). Dir: *Anthony Mann*. Cast: *June Allyson, Frank Lovejoy, Barry Sullivan, Alex Nicol, James Millican, Bruce Bennett*. 114 mins.

THE MAN FROM LARAMIE (1955). Dir: *Anthony Mann*. Cast: *Arthur Kennedy, Donald Crisp, Cathy O'Donnell, Alex Nicol, Aline MacMahon, Wallace Ford*. 104 mins.

THE MAN WHO KNEW TOO MUCH (1956). Dir: *Alfred Hitchcock*. Cast: *Doris Day, Brenda de Banzie, Bernard Miles, Ralph Truman, Daniel Gelin*. 120 mins.

THE SPIRIT OF ST. LOUIS (1957). Dir: *Billy Wilder*. Cast: *Murray Hamilton, Patricia Smith, Barlett Robinson, Marc Connelly, Arthur Space*. 135 mins.

NIGHT PASSAGE (1957). Dir: *James Neilson.* Cast: *Audie Murphy, Dan Duryea, Dianne Foster, Elaine Stewart, Brandon de Wilde, Jay C.Flippen.* 90 mins.

VERTIGO (1958). Dir: *Alfred Hitchcock.* Cast: *Kim Novak, Barbara Bel Geddes, Tom Helmore, Henry Jones, Raymond Bailey, Ellen Corby, Lee Patrick.* 128 mins.

BELL, BOOK AND CANDLE (1958). Dir: *Richard Quine.* Cast: *Kim Novak, Jack Lemmon, Ernie Kovacs, Hermoine Gingold, Elsa Lachester, Janice Rule.* 103 mins.

ANATOMY OF A MURDER (1959). Dir: *Otto Preminger.* Cast: *Lee Remick, Ben Gazzara, Joseph N.Welch, Kathryn Grant, Arthur O'Connell, Eve Arden, George C.Scott.* 160 mins.

THE FBI STORY (1959). Dir: *Mervyn LeRoy.* Cast: *Vera Miles, Murray Hamilton, Larry Pennell, Nick Adams, Diane Jergens, Jean Willes, Joyce Taylor.* 149 mins.

THE MOUNTAIN ROAD (1960). Dir: *Daniel Mann.* Cast: *Lisa Lu, Glenn Corbett, Henry Morgan, Frank Silvera, James Best, Rudy Bond, Mike Kellin.* 102 mins.

TWO RODE TOGETHER (1961). Dir: *John Ford.* Cast: *Richard Widmark, Shirley Jones, Linda Cristal, Andy Devine, John McIntire, Paul Birch, Willis Bouchey.* 109 mins.

THE MAN WHO SHOT LIBERTY VALANCE (1962). Dir: *John Ford.* Cast: *John Wayne, Vera Miles, Lee Marvin, Edmond O'Brien, Andy Devine, John Carradine.* 122 mins.

MR HOBBS TAKES A VACATION (1962). Dir: *Henry Koster.* Cast: *Maureen O'Hara, Fabian, Lauri Peters, Lili Gentle, John Saxon, John McGiver.* 116 mins.

HOW THE WEST WAS WON (1962). Dir: *Henry Hathaway.* Cast: *Carroll Baker, Karl Malden, Agnes Moorehead, Walter Brennan, Brigid Bazlen.* 162 mins.

TAKE HER, SHE'S MINE (1963). Dir: *Henry Koster.* Cast: *Sandra Dee, Audrey Meadows, Robert Morley, Philippe Forquet, John McGiver.* 98 mins.

CHEYENNE AUTUMN (1964). Dir: *John Ford.* Cast: *Arthur Kennedy, Elizabeth Allen, John Carradine, Judson Pratt, Ken Curtis, Shug Fisher.* 161 mins.

DEAR BRIGITTE (1965). Dir: *Henry Koster.* Cast: *Fabian, Glynis Johns, Cindy Carol, Billy Mumy, John Williams, Jack Kruschen, Ed Wynn, Brigitte Bardot.* 100 mins.

SHENANDOAH (1965). Dir: *Andrew V. McLaglen.* Cast: *Doug McClure, Glenn Corbett, Patrick Wayne, Rosemary Forsyth, Phillip Alford, Katharine Ross.* 105 mins.

THE FLIGHT OF THE PHOENIX (1965). Dir: *Robert Aldrich*. Cast: *Richard Attenborough, Peter Finch, Hardy Kruger, Ernest Borgnine, Ian Bannen*. 147 mins.

THE RARE BREED (1966). Dir: *Andrew V. McLaglen*. Cast: *Maureen O'Hara, Brian Keith, Juliet Mills, Don Galloway, David Brian, Jack Elam, Ben Johnson*. 97 mins.

FIRECREEK (1967). Dir: *Vincent McEveety*. Cast: *Henry Fonda, Inger Stevens, Gary Lockwood, Ed Begley, Dean Jagger, Jay C. Flippen, Jack Elam, James Best*. 104 mins.

BANDOLERO! (1968). Dir: *Andrew V. McLaglen*. Cast: *Dean Martin, Raquel Welch, George Kennedy, Andrew Prine, Will Geer, Clint Ritchie, Denver Pyle*. 106 mins.

THE CHEYENNE SOCIAL CLUB (1970). Dir: *Gene Kelly*. Cast: *Henry Fonda, Shirley Jones, Sue Ann Langdon, Elaine Devry, Robert Middleton, Arch Johnson*. 103 mins.

FOOLS' PARADE (1971). Dir: *Andrew V. McLaglen*. Cast: *George Kennedy, Anne Baxter, Strother Martin, Kurt Russell, William Windom, Mike Kellin*. 98 mins.

THE SHOOTIST (1976). Dir: *Don Siegel*. Cast: *John Wayne, Lauren Bacall, Ron Howard, Richard Boone, Hugh O'Brian, Harry Morgan, John Carradine*. 100 mins.

AIRPORT '77 (1977). Dir: *Jerry Jameson*. Cast: *Jack Lemmon, Lee Grant, Brenda Vaccaro, Joseph Cotten, Olivia de Havilland, Christopher Lee*. 114 mins.

THE BIG SLEEP (1978). Dir: *Michael Winner*. Cast: *Robert Mitchum, Sarah Miles, Richard Boone, Candy Clark, Joan Collins, John Mills*. 99 mins.

THE MAGIC OF LASSIE (1978). Dir: *Don Chaffey*. Cast: *Mickey Rooney, Alice Faye, Pernell Roberts, Stephanie Zimbalist, Michael Sharrett*. 99 mins.

THE GREEN HORIZON (1981). Dir: *Susumu Hani, Simon Trevor*. Cast: *Philip Sayer, Kathy (Cathleen McOsker), Eleonora Vallone, Hakuta Simba*. 120 mins.

Short Films and other work

ART TROUBLE (1934). 20 minute short.

IMPORTANT NEWS (1936). 10 minute short.

FELLOW AMERICANS (1942). Documentary. 10 mins.

WINNING YOUR WAYS (1942). Office of War Information Short.

THE AMERICAN CREED (1946).

THUNDERBOLT (1947). Documentary. 44 mins.

10,000 KIDS AND A COP (1948).

HOW MUCH DO YOU OWE? (1949). Documentary for Disabled American Veterans. 9 mins.

AND THEN THERE WERE FOUR (1950). Documentary on road safety. 27 mins.

AMBASSADORS WITH WINGS (1958). 25 mins.

X-15 (1961). Drama narrated by Stewart. 106 mins.

DIRECTED BY JOHN FORD (1971).

THE AMERICAN WEST OF JOHN FORD (1971).

PAT NIXON: PORTRAIT OF A FIRST LADY (1972).

THAT'S ENTERTAINMENT (1974). Co-narrator. 127 mins.

SENTIMENTAL JOURNEY (1976). 40th anniversary Documentary on DC-3 Aircraft. 20 mins.

Television Credits

As well as the following select chronology Stewart has been a guest star in The Dean Martin Show, The Jack Benny Show, The Julie Andrews Show, Parkinson, Stars on Sunday etc.

THE WINDMILL (1955). Cast: *Barbara Hale, Donald MacDonald, Cheryl Callaway, John McIntire, Walter Sande, James Millican, Edgar Buchanan*. 30 mins.

THE TOWN WITHOUT A PASS (1957). Cast: *Fredd Wayne, Walter Sande, Ted Mapes*. Introduced by Ronald Reagan. 30 mins.

THE TRAIL TO CHRISTMAS (1957). Cast: *Richard Eyer, John McIntire, Sam Edwards, Will Wright, Kevin Hagen, Sally Frazier*. (Dir: *James Stewart*). 30 mins.

FLASHING SPIKES (1962). Cast: *Jack Warden, Pat Wayne, Edgar Buchanan, Tige Andrews, Carleton Young, Willis Bouchey, Don Drysdale*. (Dir: *John Ford*). 53 mins.

THE JIMMY STEWART SHOW (1971). Dir: *Hal Kanter*. 24 Episodes.

HARVEY (1972). Cast: *Helen Hayes, Marian Mailey, John McGiver, Richard Mulligan, Jesse White, Arlene Francis, Madeline Kahn*. (Dir: *Fielder Cook*). 90 mins.

HAWKINS ON MURDER (1973). Eight feature-length episodes.

MR KRUEGER'S CHRISTMAS (1980). Cast: *The Mormon Tabernacle Choir*. 30 mins.

RIGHT OF WAY (1983). Cast: *Bette Davis, Melinda Dillon, Priscilla Morrill, John Harkins, Louis Schaefer, Jacque Lynn Colton*. (Dir: *George Schaefer*). 106 mins.

Stage Work

1932: *Magnolia. It's A Wise Child. Carrie Nation. Goodbye Again.*
1933: *Camille.* (stage manager). *Spring in Autumn. All Good Americans.*
1934: *Yellow Jack. Divided By Three. Page Miss Glory.*
1935: *Journey By Night.*
1947: *Harvey*
1948: *Harvey*
1970: *Harvey*
1975: *Harvey* (in London).

Select Bibliography

Peter Bogdanovich **Picture Shows** (London, George Allen & Unwin, 1975)
Allen Eyles **James Stewart** (London, W.H.Allen, 1984)
A.E.Hotchner **Doris Day: Her Own Story**
(London, W.H.Allen, 1976)
Joshua Logan **Josh: My Up and Down, In and Out Life**
(London, W.H.Allen, 1977)
Arthur F.McClure
Ken D.Jones &
Alfred E. Twomey **The Films of James Stewart**
(London, Thomas Yoseloff, 1970)
Cobbett Steinberg **Reel Facts** (London, Penguin, 1981)
Howard Teichman **Fonda: My Life as told to Howard Teichman**
(London, W.H.Allen, 1982)
Howard Thompson **James Stewart** (New York, Pyramid
Communications, 1974)